GUTS & GLORY

WORLD WAR II

GUTS & GLORY
WORLD WAR II

BEN THOMPSON

ILLUSTRATIONS BY
C. M. BUTZER

Little, Brown and Company
New York Boston

Little, Brown and Company

Hachette Book Group
1290 Avenue of the Americas, New York, NY 10104
Visit us at lb-kids.com

Little, Brown and Company is a division of Hachette Book Group, Inc.
The Little, Brown name and logo are trademarks of Hachette Book Group, Inc.

The publisher is not responsible for websites (or their content) that are not owned by the publisher.

First Edition: March 2016

Library of Congress Cataloging-in-Publication Data

Thompson, Ben, 1980–
Guts & glory: World War II / Ben Thompson ; illustrations by C. M. Butzer.
pages cm. — (Guts & glory ; 3)
Includes bibliographical references and index.
Audience: Ages 8–12.
ISBN 978-0-316-32059-7 (hardcover) — ISBN 978-0-316-32060-3 (ebook) —
ISBN 978-0-316-32199-0 (library edition ebook) 1. World War, 1939–1945—Juvenile literature.
I. Butzer, C. M., illustrator. II. Title. III. Title: World War II.
D743.7.T54 2016
940.54—dc23
2015012917

10 9 8 7 6 5 4 3 2 1

RRD-C

Printed in the United States of America

YOU ARE HERE TODAY
FOR THREE REASONS.

FIRST,
BECAUSE YOU ARE HERE
TO DEFEND YOUR HOMES AND
YOUR LOVED ONES.

SECOND,
YOU ARE HERE FOR YOUR OWN
SELF-RESPECT, BECAUSE YOU
WOULD NOT WANT TO BE
ANYWHERE ELSE.

THIRD,
YOU ARE HERE BECAUSE
YOU ARE REAL MEN AND
ALL REAL MEN LIKE TO FIGHT.

—General George S. Patton, Commander,
US Third Army

CONTENTS

The battlefront disappeared, and with it the illusion that there had ever been a battlefront. For this was no war of occupation, but a war of quick penetration and obliteration—Blitzkrieg, Lightning War.

—*TIME* magazine, September 25, 1939

Introduction 1

Author's Note 15

1. Eight Hundred Heroes 19

In the opening hours of World War II, a lone battalion of Chinese soldiers hold their position in a bombed-out warehouse against the rampaging Japanese army.

INTRODUCTION

My good friends, for the second time in our history, a British prime minister has returned from Germany bringing peace with honor. I believe it is peace for our time. We thank you from the bottom of our hearts. Go home and get a nice quiet sleep.

—British prime minister Neville Chamberlain, September 30, 1938

ON JUNE 28, 1919, THE LEADERS OF FRANCE, Germany, Great Britain, and the United States met at an old palace outside Paris and signed the Treaty of Versailles, marking the official end of the First World War (which was just called the Great War before we had a second world war to compare it to—more on this in chapter 2). It had been the bloodiest and most brutal war in human history, leaving millions dead and ruining cities and lands all across

Europe. For the most part the war had been a draw, with both sides losing a ridiculous number of men for very little gain. But in the end, Germany's government was the one that finally collapsed in 1918, and it was replaced with guys who decided it made sense to stop fighting and end this horrible thing once and for all.

The Allied powers, particularly France, were eager to make sure Germany suffered for starting such a terrible war. So the terms of the treaty were more lopsided than a gorilla sitting on a teeter-totter. Big chunks of Germany were cut out and given to France, Denmark, Poland, and Belgium. Germans weren't allowed to have an army bigger than a hundred thousand guys, and they couldn't have warplanes, tanks, or new battleships. They had to pay crazy huge amounts of cash to France and Britain, and sanctions and bills were imposed on them that would cripple any economy on earth.

German money became worthless. Factories closed. People lost their jobs. The country fell into poverty and depression. So you can imagine that to the German people, the terms of the deal were majorly harsh. Sure, they'd surrendered, but they hadn't really "lost." No Allied soldiers had even set foot in Germany during the war. Plus, when the Germans were thinking about surrendering, the Allies had promised they'd go easy on them. And now this? What gives?

Into this situation stepped a man now pretty much universally accepted as the most evil person in history: Adolf Hitler.

A failed artist from Austria who had served as a corporal in World War I, Hitler was, let's say, a *little upset* that Germany got the short end of the stick in the Treaty of Versailles. Looking at the once-proud German people suffering made him so angry that he wanted to kill basically everyone in the world.

Hitler was convinced that the leadership of Germany was weak and that the German people had been undermined by Jews and other groups of people he didn't like. Swearing to reverse the Treaty of Versailles, throw the Jews out, retake the lands Germany had lost, and bring the country back to the ranks of world powers, Hitler tried to overthrow the government in 1923 but was defeated and arrested. While in jail, he wrote a book about his beliefs, and before long it was circulating among unhappy Germans.

By 1933 Hitler had been released from jail and had become so popular that he was elected chancellor of Germany. When the president of Germany died a few months later, Hitler merged both offices under the title of *Führer* (which means "leader"), put himself in that office, and assumed total control over the German population.

His first move was to abolish every single political party other than his own, which was called the National Socialist German Workers' Party (better known as the Nazis). Using a combination of powerful speeches, terrorizing secret police forces, and a mega-bombardment of "Nazis are awesome"

German soldiers watching Hitler speak at a rally in Nuremberg, 1935

propaganda, Hitler worked to undermine the Treaty of Versailles step-by-step. In 1935 he declared he was going to build weapons whether France wanted him to or not. In 1936 he moved troops into the Rhineland demilitarized zone (a section of Germany with no army or weapons allowed), hosted the Olympics (awarding Germany a ton of gold medals for all kinds of dumb things), sent troops to fight in the Spanish Civil War, and started hardcore cracking down on the rights of Jews living in Germany. Then in 1938 he absorbed Austria into his lands, which was fine with Austria because they were super into it.

Now, the British and the French weren't all that pumped up about the idea of going into another long, bloody war with Germany, so for the most part they offered pretty lame opposition. When Hitler decided he wanted to annex (absorb) Czechoslovakia, the prime minister of Britain, Neville Chamberlain, met with Hitler, talked it over, and was like, "Okay, well, I guess you can have it, but only if you promise to stop annexing countries." And Hitler was like, "Okay, yeah, sure, sounds good, buddy, whatever you say." Then Chamberlain flew home to tell everyone that all wars were over forever, so hooray.

A year later, Hitler launched an all-out, unprovoked attack on Poland with one goal in mind: complete domination and conquest.

Britain and France declared war immediately.

Adolph Hitler, 1937

By the time the war was over, almost two billion people from more than sixty countries would take up arms in conflicts raging from Cairo, Egypt, to Unalaska, Alaska (yes, there is an Alaskan island called Unalaska, which I guess must have been discovered on Opposite Day or something). Sixty million people would be dead and wounded in just six years, including thirty-five million innocent civilians. Atrocities would be committed on never-before-seen scales. Cities would be leveled. Nuclear weapons would be deployed.

This is the story of World War II.

THE ARMIES (WELL, THE "MAIN" ARMIES)

Since we're dealing with a conflict involving basically every single country on the face of the earth, it probably makes sense to give you a little help wrapping your head around what the heck is going on with this big, confusing war.

THE AXIS POWERS

Nazi Germany

The German Reich (which means "empire") was a militant, totalitarian dictatorship ruled with an iron fist by that Adolf Hitler guy I just talked about. Hitler won complete political power over all of Germany by running on a platform that basically asked "Who else hates Jews?" By the start of World War II, Hitler had rebuilt Germany into an industrialized, powerful country with bleeding-edge military technology and fanatical squads of well-trained soldiers ready to lay their lives on the line without a moment's hesitation. Hitler held absolute power over every aspect of German life, right down to (I kid you not) creating pamphlets telling blond teenage girls what type of boys they should go out on dates with. German forces had advanced tactics, an impressive fleet of powerful tanks, and veteran attack pilots who had been battling Communists in the Spanish Civil War for the past two years. They were ready to conquer the world.

The Kingdom of Italy

Italy fought with the Allies (more on them in a minute) during World War I, but in the years between the two world wars, the country fell into political and economic chaos. Intense arguments and street fighting were going on between everyone from anarchists (people who want no government) to monarchists (people who want a superpowerful king in charge). Into this crazy, swirling mass of screaming and punching Italian dudes came Benito Mussolini, a schoolteacher, a propaganda newspaper editor, and a World War I veteran who founded the Italian Fascist Party in 1919. Mussolini promised that if people made him the absolute dictator of Italy, he'd bring the country back to the good old days of ancient Rome, and most people thought that sounded pretty good. The people who didn't were beaten up in the streets by gangs of goons known as Blackshirts. Mussolini took over in 1922—eleven years before Hitler did in Germany—getting the king of Italy, Victor Emmanuel III, to grant him total control of everything. By 1925 everyone was just calling Mussolini *Il Duce*, meaning "the Leader." He did such a good job of being a tyrant that Hitler looked up to him as a role model for how to completely dominate your society like a supervillain overseeing his minions. Mussolini attacked Abyssinia (modern-day Ethiopia) and Albania in the 1930s, but his population and army were unmotivated and disorganized, so that didn't go so well. These problems persisted, and later in the war, he constantly had to rely on Hitler and the Germans to bail him out of sticky situations.

The Empire of Japan

Japan was a dominant empire on land and on the sea, with a powerful central government, millions of people, and a modern, highly industrialized society. The people were unswervingly loyal to their emperor, Hirohito, and most believed him to be a living god on earth. Just seventy years earlier, this take-no-prisoners warrior culture was fighting within itself with samurai swords. But in the time since, it had quickly scaled up to become the dominant force in Asia.

The Japanese didn't have a lot of natural materials like oil or steel or food for their large population, so they typically had to rely on trade to get enough of these things. But they believed that they were the world's superior race and that it was their national destiny to take what they needed from weaker civilizations. In 1905 they shocked the world by soundly defeating Russia in combat—the first time an Asian country had defeated a

European one in war since the days of Genghis Khan. In 1910 they invaded Korea, conquered it, enslaved large parts of the population, and forbade anyone to speak the Korean language. In 1931 they did a similar thing to the Chinese province of Manchuria. At the time of World War II, they were led by Prime Minister Hideki Tojo, an angry, warlike dude who couldn't wait to keep expanding the country through military full-court domination.

THE ALLIES

The British Empire

In 1939 the British Empire had direct power over 25 percent of planet Earth. Centered in the United Kingdom and ruled by King George VI, the Empire included the countries of England, Scotland, Wales, Northern Ireland, Canada, Australia, New Zealand, and South Africa. Beyond that, the British also controlled Egypt, India, Singapore, and huge chunks of Southeast Asia, southern Africa, and the Middle East. They had the strongest navy on earth and could call on tens of millions of troops at a moment's notice. However, World War I had been kind of a sore spot for these guys, and nobody in Britain was all that excited about getting involved in another planet-spanning war. The prime minister, Neville Chamberlain, did everything he could to try to let Hitler do his own thing, but as the conflict heated up, Chamberlain was thrown out of office in favor of his biggest political opponent: Winston Churchill. This guy was an awesome, crotchety old cigar-chomper known as the "British Bulldog." Churchill had been a cavalryman in Africa and was First Lord of the Admiralty early on during World War I, and he was determined to fight as hard as he possibly could against the scourge of Hitler.

The Republic of France

Despite losing millions of soldiers in World War I, France defeated Germany, but the fighting had all taken place on French soil and the country suffered horribly. So the French seriously hated the Germans' guts and were ready to smack down Hitler at any price. By 1940 France had rebuilt one of the largest and best-equipped armies in the world, with nearly six million soldiers standing ready. They were backed by tanks and warplanes, all situated along the Maginot Line—a crazy network of concrete forts, barbed wire, and impenetrable bases that spanned the length of the France-Germany border. They didn't want to fight, but they were ready.

The Union of Soviet Socialist Republics

The USSR was made up of fifteen republics from Ukraine to present-day Kazakhstan, all unified under the general control of Russia, which was the largest and most influential of the republics. The Russians (it's not technically accurate to call people from the Soviet Union

"Russians," but we do it anyway) had an all-powerful king known as the tsar (pronounced "zar") until 1918, when a bunch of Communists whacked him and seized power. (The beginning of the movie *Anastasia* is supposed to show how this happened, but it wasn't actually like that in real life.) Afterward, the USSR was ruled by Josef Stalin, a ferocious dictator who used brutal measures to industrialize and modernize his country. Millions died from his forced relocations and straight-up executions, and anyone who had a problem with him had a nasty habit of disappearing in the middle of the night and waking up in a freezing cold Siberian tundra work camp.

In the late 1930s, Stalin (a name that literally means "Iron Man") freaked out and got mad at his own political party and military, mostly because he was power-hungry and totally paranoid. He had popular Communist leader Leon Trotsky assassinated, massacred large portions of his political cabinet, and ordered the execution of over two-thirds of the generals in the Soviet Red Army. This was not really a smart move, as Stalin found out in 1939 when he tried to conquer Finland and lost almost half of his attacking force because there wasn't anyone competent to lead them. But despite losing hundreds of thousands of troops, the Soviets eventually defeated Finland and began the process of training new leadership. They had very little industry, equipment, or commanders at the beginning of World War II, but they were a huge country and had more soldiers than almost all the Axis powers combined.

The United States of America

The United States had suffered immensely from the Great Depression, which began in 1929 and lasted a terrible ten years, so most Americans weren't interested in going all the way across the Atlantic to get shot at. There was a big movement saying that the best thing to do was to stay out of this mess and let Europe deal with its problems while the United States fixed its own issues. President Franklin D. Roosevelt instituted several plans to get people working and to rebuild the economy, set strategies in motion to build up American defenses just in case, and started a program called lend-lease in which the United States built war material and made extra cash selling them to the United Kingdom and to the USSR. Hitler wasn't a big fan of this, but both Germany and Japan saw the States as a "sleeping giant" and didn't want to get America involved in the war unless they really had to. The United States was at a disadvantage because it was so far away from all the fighting, but it had a crazy-powerful industrial sector that allowed it to build more tanks, aircraft, and vehicles than anyone else in the world.

AUTHOR'S NOTE

> **Victory at all costs, victory in spite of all terror, victory however long and hard the road may be; for without victory, there is no survival.**
>
> —British prime minister Winston Churchill, May 13, 1940

WHERE DO YOU BEGIN WHEN YOU'RE TRYING to write a history of World War II? If just about every civilization on earth is involved in an epic, continent-spanning bloodbath that goes on for five-plus years and kills more people than any other military action in human history, how do you trim that down into twenty chapters?

It took me about six weeks just to figure out where the heck to start. Trying to balance three major theaters of operation (East, West, and Pacific) in a way that was going to be interesting and informative without leaving out a key battle or detail that changes the course of history isn't easy (not to mention the fact that just about every single battle involves some kind of horrific event that *has* to be dealt with tactfully). How do you talk about the Holocaust, the atomic bomb, the Japanese sack of Nanjing, or the many other massive civilian casualty events without completely ruining the fun and thrill of a book about daring feats of heroic bravery?

My goal in writing this book has been to touch on major themes, key battles, and significant events from the history of World War II. I wanted to follow the war from its beginnings in Manchuria to its end on the USS *Missouri* while still trying to keep it exciting and super-packed with action. It's beyond the scope of the Guts & Glory series to get too far into the horrors that took place during this brutal and divisive war, but we can't ignore some of the hardest and most important lessons that humanity learned during the 1930s and 1940s. So I've presented certain ones without pulling any punches, and I encourage readers to dig into primary source material on the subjects and learn more.

By that same token, while human beings are capable of some truly terrible things, we are also capable of incredible heroism, bravery, compassion, and honor. The people of World War II routinely faced overwhelming odds, gritted their teeth, and charged headlong into life-threatening danger to defend their families, their homes, and their beliefs. They put their bodies on the line to help those in need. They unflinchingly pushed themselves to the limit even when all hope seemed lost. And they did it not because they were too dumb to give up, but because they were smart enough to know that nothing is ever truly impossible.

Those are the stories I've chosen to highlight in this book—the true tales of unrivaled heroism in the face of unbelievably, ridiculously terrible odds. I hope they inspire you the way they've inspired me.

1

EIGHT HUNDRED HEROES

The Battle of Sihang Warehouse

Shanghai, Republic of China
October 26–November 1, 1937

We will fight the enemy with our last bullet, and will punish him with our last drop of blood. Defend to the death.

—Colonel Xie Jinyuan, Chinese Nationalist Army

THE CONSTANT CRACK OF RIFLE FIRE AND THE rumbling of armored cars echoed through the black smoke hanging in the night air. Shanghai, the fifth-largest city in the world, was burning. It had once been known as "the Queen of the Orient," a glitzy metropolis of high fashion, luxurious nightlife, bustling harbors, and towering skyscrapers. It was now rapidly being reduced to a mixture of bloody hand-dug trenches, empty bullet casings, and coiled tangles of barbed wire. The city of Shanghai had been home to three and a half million civilians. Now it was the front line of what would become the biggest and most destructive war in human history.

Amid the chaos and epic horribleness, Colonel Xie Jinyuan of the Chinese Nationalist Army calmly walked toward the imposing headquarters of his shattered division. The steel-and-concrete rectangular building known as the Sihang Warehouse was one of the few surviving structures amid the rubble of northern Shanghai. It was sturdy and secure; it backed against the Suzhou River and would be the perfect defensive position. Exhausted from three months of nonstop combat against a determined, unrelenting enemy, Xie Jinyuan decided that he and the surviving members of his command would make their last stand here.

A lot of uptight, pipe-smoking historians like to go on and on about how World War II started with Adolf Hitler's invasion of Poland in 1939, mostly because they don't think it's cool to pay attention to any history that didn't happen in Europe or the United States. In reality, the first shots of World War II were fired in 1937 when the swiftly growing empire of Japan decided to flex its bulging muscles by conquering everything around it. Fueled by its people's fanatical devotion to their emperor, their unequaled ferocity in battle, and some of the

most advanced military technology this side of a science-fiction movie, Japan defeated Russia in a war in 1905, annexed Korea in 1910, and captured the province of Manchuria from China in 1932. In 1937 the Japanese war machine surged forward once again, this time with a full-scale attack into the heart of China itself.

The Chinese were in the middle of a civil war at the time, making it really inconsiderate of the Japanese to start bombing them while they were busy trying to kill one another. The uncoordinated, unprepared frontline armies of China were churned into mulch and lost their capital city, Beijing, to the Japanese pretty much immediately. By October, what remained of the Chinese military was falling back toward the Yangtze River and the important port city of Shanghai.

Chinese soldiers defending Shanghai, 1937

With more than a hundred thousand elite Japanese troops storming toward them, the Chinese prepared to dig in and defend their city at all costs. They had way more fighters than the Japanese, but they were not nearly as well trained or as well equipped. Shanghai quickly became a war zone, with defenders digging five-foot-deep trenches in the middle of streets while Japanese bombers reduced skyscrapers to smoking ruins. Homes were flattened, factories were gutted, and the biggest battle to grip Asia in over a century swept the economic heartland of China with fire and bullets.

By the time Xie Jinyuan moved his troops into the Sihang Warehouse on October 26, 1937, it was pretty much all over. The Chinese had fought bravely, but they were outmatched in every way. A few days earlier, a flotilla of Japanese warships had pulled into the harbor, rained gunfire on the city, and then deployed hardcore Japanese marines right behind the main lines of the Chinese troops, all but cutting off their escape route. The command came down for the Chinese army to retreat from the city and evacuate as many civilians as possible in the process.

The specific orders given to Colonel Xie were simple: Hold the warehouse until someone kills you. Buy the civilians and soldiers of Shanghai time to get the heck out of there before the Japanese level the city into a giant pile of smoking misery. Make the invaders pay for every step.

Sihang Warehouse was the perfect spot to defend. Standing out like a beacon amid the destruction of the Battle of Shanghai, the six-story warehouse was made of bulletproof concrete and had plenty of good spots for sniper rifle hide-and-seek. Better yet, it was positioned across a narrow river from a part of

Shanghai known as the International Settlement—a neighborhood that was home to British, French, and American embassies and citizens. The Japanese couldn't bomb the warehouse to cinder blocks with artillery and airplanes, because if just one little bomb missed its target and accidentally landed on some British guy's house, the Japanese would have an ugly international incident on their hands. They were going to have to take this warehouse the old-fashioned way if they wanted to get rid of Xie and his battalion.

Thirty-two-year-old Colonel Xie Jinyuan was a graduate of China's Whampoa Military Academy (later renamed the Central Military Academy), and the men of his battalion were some of the best troops the Chinese military had to offer. Kitted out with top-of-the-line German helmets, rifles, and other gear, these guys had been hand-trained by General Alexander von Falkenhausen, an awesome-looking old German military commander who had fought against the British in World War I and had earned his country's highest award for military bravery. Xie knew he was outnumbered and outgunned and had no hope of reinforcement, resupply, or survival. But he didn't even flinch—he went right to work, preparing to give the Japanese the fight of their lives. He ordered his men to clear out the areas around the warehouse so they'd have open lines of fire. He looted surrounding warehouses and shops for food, ammo, and medical supplies. He rigged nearby buildings with explosives so he could blow them up if the Japanese tried to set up snipers or machine guns inside them. He had his men cut holes in the ten-foot-thick walls of the warehouse so they could shoot through them while staying behind cover. Sure, this was an unwinnable battle, but Xie Jinyuan and his soldiers were determined to show the world that China wasn't going down without a fight.

The Japanese arrived on the morning of October 27. The attack began at dawn.

The job of kicking down the warehouse fell to the soldiers of Japan's elite Third Division, who rolled up with mortars (potato-gun-looking tubes used to launch bombs short distances), machine guns, and armored cars. As the men of the Third Division approached the warehouse, they were greeted by a high five of Chinese bullets all up in their grills. Colonel Xie's troops were battle-hardened warriors, and they had spent the past three months defending a train station in the northern part of town. That battle had reduced their forces from 800 to 414, but the soldiers who remained were excellent marksmen and weren't about to freak out just because the Japanese were raking their warehouse with a nonstop stream of machine-gun bullets and other deadly objects.

The battle lasted most of the day, with the Japanese attacking many times. Colonel Xie ran up and down, screaming for his men to hold the line. At one point he even had to run downstairs with a bucket of water and a rifle because a couple of Japanese dudes broke into the warehouse and tried to set a fire in the room where Xie kept some of his bullets and fuel (which would have been pretty bad for him).

The Japanese attack halted that night, and Xie used the break to have his men rebuild the defenses and move their guns to different hiding spots. He even snuck a couple of his wounded men across the bridge to the British side so they could get medical attention.

The next morning, Xie looked out the window and saw an interesting sight—all along the British side of the river were people standing and watching the fight. British soldiers, international journalists, and even Chinese residents of Shanghai who had escaped to safety in the International Settlement were lined up to watch and cheer on the brave defenders of Sihang Warehouse.

One of the people lining the banks of the river was a girl named Yang Huimin. She watched in awe as the defenders spent yet another day fighting off nonstop attacks from the Japanese, shooting apart attempts to storm the building and raining down grenades and mortar fire on Japanese tanks that tried to roll up on the structure.

For Yang, only one thing was missing: The Chinese defenders didn't have a flag over their building. So that night, when the fighting stopped, she wrapped a Chinese Nationalist flag around herself, swam across the Suzhou River, and snuck into the building. By the next morning, Yang had already escaped back to the British side of the river, and the Japanese woke up to a giant Chinese flag staring them in the face. This made them even crankier.

For an incredible four days, the brave warriors of Sihang Warehouse held out against pretty much everything the Japanese Third Division had to offer. The 414 men (known to the international press as "the Eight Hundred Heroes" because Xie lied about how many guys he had with him) fought day and night, with no break from the constant Japanese onslaught. When the Japanese turned off the building's running water, the Chinese collected their pee in big gross buckets and used that to put out fires. When the Japanese put mortars and machine guns on opposing roofs, Xie blew them up with accurate mortar fire. When the Japanese drove tanks up to the front door of the warehouse, guys laid their lives on the line to attack them with hand grenades. When enemy teams broke into the lower floors of the structure, Chinese troops met them head-on with bayonets and face punches until the Japanese got out. For seventy-two seemingly endless hours, the Eight Hundred Heroes struggled for their lives, firing so many bullets that the barrels of their guns turned orange from the heat.

Xie had been ordered to defend to the death, but on November 1 his commanders told him to go—the city was evacuated and the mission was complete. So in the very late hours of the day, Xie had his men make a break for the river, leaving behind a few badly wounded soldiers to lay down covering fire with heavy machine guns. Xie and the 376 survivors of the battle reached the British side, where they would end up being confined for the next three years. For the first heroes of World War II, the war was over before it had really gotten started.

The Eight Hundred Heroes became superstars overnight. Despite the defeat at Shanghai and the destruction of the main Chinese military, the tale of Colonel Xie and his brave men inspired the Chinese people to carry on the battle and resist the Japanese takeover in any way they could.

NAZIS IN THE HIMALAYAS?

On a weird note, the Japanese invasion of China annoyingly messed up Nazi plans to travel to Tibet in search of a secret race of white-skinned supermen. Yes, you read that correctly. In 1937 a world-renowned German adventurer and zoologist named Ernst Schäfer left Berlin to explore Tibet and document its wildlife, ecology, and botany. But many folks aren't quite sure that's the whole reason he was traveling there. Schäfer was a pretty legit scientist, but most of the money for this trip was put up by Heinrich Himmler, the head of a super-nefarious Nazi organization known as the SS (find more about this in chapter 10). Himmler not only saw this mission as an opportunity to put photos of heroic-looking, mountain-climbing Nazis on the front page of the news, but also is believed to have ordered Schäfer to search for anything from Indiana Jones–style magical devices to hidden races of white guys who had lived in the Himalayas for centuries. The British were pretty sure he was just scouting out the best trails to use to attack India from China, so they tried to block him from entering Tibet. But the enterprising German went around the Japan-China war, snuck past the Brits, and spent fourteen months climbing the Himalayas, gathering data and talking to the locals. Schäfer returned with journals packed full of notes on everything from Buddhist rituals to Himalayan wasp ecology, but he never mentioned anything about world-destroying ancient artifacts or Abominable Snowmen.

THE FALL OF NANJING

After the fall of Shanghai, the Japanese pushed farther south to Nanjing, which at the time was the capital of the Chinese Nationalists under Chiang Kai-Shek. The Japanese were not kind to the city. They killed everyone they found and looted and destroyed everything they could. Current estimates suggest that three hundred thousand innocent civilians were butchered in a truly horrifying display that causes trouble between the two countries to this day. Amid the carnage and misery, one man, a prominent Nazi Party member named John Rabe, used whatever powers he could to shelter people from the destruction. Rabe is credited with protecting as many as two hundred thousand people from Japanese brutality in Nanjing.

PUTTING THE CIVIL WAR ON PAUSE

China was ruled by emperors for more than three thousand years, but when the last emperor of the Qing Dynasty was overthrown in 1911, there was a big, nasty debate over how the country should be run. This eventually blew up into the 1927 Chinese Civil War, during which a pro-democracy military dictator named Chiang Kai-Shek fought against Communist forces under Chairman Mao Zedong. When Japan rolled tanks and warplanes into town, the two Chinese leaders agreed to stop shooting each other until they'd defeated the Japanese, and for the most part both sides held up their end of the deal. But after Japan was finally thrown out in 1945, the two dictators picked up right where they'd left off. Mao Zedong won the war and set up the Communist People's Republic of China on October 1, 1949. Chiang and his troops fled to the island of Taiwan, and the government they established there holds power to this day. Needless to say, China and Taiwan still pretty much mega-hate each other.

HIROMICHI SHINOHARA

Expansion through China brought the Japanese up against the border of Russia, and in 1939 the Japanese and the Soviet Union had a short but insanely bloody war in the skies above the Mongolia-Russia border. Hiromichi Shinohara was a young, eagle-eyed cavalry officer who traded in his horse for a Nakajima Ki-27 "Nate" fighter plane, and he was such a master of air-to-air combat that he shot down four enemy fighter planes in his very first combat mission. Once he got the hang of it, he got *really* good, and on his second mission (the very next day) he became a fighter "ace in a day" by shooting down five Russian I-15 fighter planes in a single mission. Sure, the dinky old I-15 is one of those ancient-style Red Baron–looking wooden biplanes with the two sets of wings, and Hiromichi was flying a much more modern single-wing fighter aircraft with heavy machine guns in the wings, but it's still a pretty mind-blowing accomplishment.

Fighting among hundreds of diving, shooting, and exploding aircraft, Hiromichi engaged in scorching battles that more closely resembled Xbox Live multiplayer death matches than something you'd expect out of a real-life World War II battle. On June 27, 1939, he dove head-on through a 150-plane brawl and shot down eleven Russians like something out of an arcade game.

Hiromichi was awesome because his primary method of attack was to hold down the trigger of his twin-linked 7.7mm machine guns and dive from the sky at three hundred miles per hour straight into the middle of enemy aircraft formations. Hiromichi's kill-or-be-killed, lone-wolf style would throw his prey into complete panic, their formation would break apart, and then he would go around shooting them one by one while they ran for their lives.

Flight Lieutenant Hiromichi Shinohara's entire military service career spanned just three months. In that short time, he managed to record confirmed air-to-air kills on an insane *fifty-eight* Russian fighter planes. He was last seen in August 1939, swarmed by enemy aircraft diving in on him from all directions. According to the report written about his death, the lieutenant managed to blow up three more enemy fighters before he was shot down and killed. He was the most successful Japanese Army Air Force pilot of World War II, and he hadn't even lived long enough to see the United States enter the conflict.

KNOW YOUR VEHICLES

	Type 89B Chi-Ro	Panzer Mark I
TYPE	Medium tank	Medium tank
COUNTRY	Japan	Germany (purchased by China)
FIRST PRODUCED	1928	1934
LENGTH	18 feet, 10 inches	13 feet
WEIGHT	14 tons	6 tons
ARMOR	17 millimeters	7 millimeters
ENGINE	120-hp Mitsubishi A6120V 6-cylinder	59-hp Krupp M305 4-cylinder
TOP SPEED	16 mph	31 mph
CREW	4	2
ARMAMENT	One Type 90 57mm cannon Two 6.5mm machine guns	Two 7.92mm machine guns

The main Japanese battle tank of the early war was basically a solid steel bunker on wheels with a machine gun and a little cannon mounted on top. The Chinese forces, on the other hand, had only a small number of German hand-me-downs that hadn't been cool for something like five years. Their small machine guns couldn't even punch through the thin Japanese tanks' armor.

2

BLITZKRIEG

Germany Conquers Europe in Ten Months

September 1, 1939–June 22, 1940
Poland and France

Gentlemen, you are about to witness the most famous victory in history.

—German Führer Adolf Hitler, in a speech to his staff on the eve of the Battle of France

IN MAY **1940** TWO OF THE WORLD'S MOST POWERFUL nations were poised for an earth-shattering battle that would morph the entire landscape of Europe into a gigantic explosion.

On paper, the battle was going to be longer, more brutal, and more grueling than trying to solve the world's most evil algebra word problem while people are shooting at you. Along the Rhine River, which forms part of the border between Germany and France, stood the German *Wehrmacht* (Germany's entire military, consisting of their air force, navy, and army), 3.35 million soldiers decked out for war. Across the river from them defiantly stood 3.3 million French and British troops, entrenched in massively impressive forts and defensive positions they'd been working on for over a decade. The Germans had a big advantage when it came to numbers of aircraft, but the Allies had twice as much artillery—fourteen thousand artillery pieces to just seven thousand German guns. The French also had nearly a thousand more tanks than Germany did, and the French tanks were more heavily armored and carried a larger main gun than the German panzer tanks.

So how did France fall in six weeks?

To understand the French defeat, you need to understand the way World War I went down. You see, just twenty years earlier these same two sides had collided head-to-head in the bloodiest conflict the world had ever witnessed. Tens of millions of men died in World War I while fighting for just a few miles of territory. Both sides suffered monumentally, and in the end, nothing had been accomplished. Troops would run across open ground and get mowed down by machine guns, and those who somehow survived would run back to their own lines to get out of the bullet streams. The guys who had just done all the killing would then be like, "Okay, cool, sweet, we wore them down" and launch an attack of their own, only to be mowed down by machine guns themselves. The whole bloody war was the military equivalent of two guys taking turns punching each other in the face really hard, and this fighting style had taught the French commanders that power lay in defense rather than in attack. The guy with the best fortress won, and the guy dumb enough to charge the fortress died. So France decided to repeat the tactics that had already defeated the Germans once: build an unrivaled line of trenches along the French-German border, pack it with hundreds of thousands of men and artillery, and wait for Germany to attack so France could waste them with machine guns.

What they hadn't planned on was the man known as "Hurricane Heinz" Guderian and his new tactic for German military success:

The blitzkrieg.

Born in Kulm, Germany, in 1888, Heinz Guderian was a staff officer during World War I, and he learned a very different lesson than the French did from that long, horrible war. Rather than sit back and chill, the key to success was to launch quick, unexpected attacks as fast as possible. Sucker punch the enemy's weak points with overwhelming might. France could dig their holes and wait, but Guderian wanted to be the guy throwing the punches, and he realized that modern technology had given him the perfect tools to lob haymakers at the French: the bomber aircraft and the battle tank.

Before Heinz Guderian, a lot of military generals would use tanks the same way they'd use a machine-gun nest: Spread them out evenly across your lines so you can have one in your area to assist at all times. Guderian thought this was dumb as heck. In 1937 he wrote a book called *Achtung—Panzer!* (which is an awesome title because it's just German for "*Attention—Tank!*"). In his book, he wrote, "You hit somebody with your fist and not with your fingers spread," and argued that the best way to do things was to slam all your tanks together into one big tank unit, rev up your engines, and then roll over top of anyone who stood in front of you. Think of it this way: "Blitzing" the quarterback in football is a reference to the blitzkrieg. If you want to get their quarterback before he can throw the ball, you need your big linebackers to run as fast as they can from directions the offense isn't expecting and nail their QB when he least expects it.

Heinz Guderian and the Germans had already had their first opportunity to test out blitzkrieg (meaning "lightning war") when they launched a full-scale invasion of Poland in September 1939. Poland's military was full of tough, dedicated soldiers, but there were 2.5 million Germans and 1,500 panzer tanks against just 280,000 Poles who were still riding around on horses because they didn't have enough trucks to carry their troops. The blitzkrieg worked with terrifying efficiency—Nazi paratroopers landed behind enemy lines and quickly took out communications and headquarters buildings, cutting off the eyes and ears of Poland's frontline forces. Aircraft from the Luftwaffe (the German air force) screamed in from overhead, shot up Polish airplanes while they were still on the tarmac, then ruthlessly dropped bombs on any ground target larger than a Porta Potty. Before the smoke could clear on all those explosions, five full-strength divisions of terrifying steel panzer tanks rolled in through the gaps, blasting high-explosive artillery shells and machine-gun bullets in every direction. The panzers used their speed to quickly surround the Polish Army and force their surrender. Despite heroic efforts from some small pockets of Polish resistance, particularly in the capital, Warsaw, the Poles were completely conquered in just under a month. Hitler celebrated by high-fiving Stalin and splitting the country between them as if they were arguing over pizza slices. (At this point in time, Hitler and Stalin were frenemies who were nice to each other's face but were totally plotting to double-cross each other at the first sign of weakness.)

During the invasion of Poland, Hurricane Heinz had commanded the Nineteenth Panzer Corps with amazing success, but he knew that the true test of blitzkrieg was going to be the battle about to take place in France.

France knew war was coming and made great efforts to defend against it. They built the Maginot Line on the

France-Germany border and made it the most impenetrable defensive position ever constructed in human history. If Germany decided to go around the defenses and attack through Holland and Belgium (as they had in World War I), France also had a plan in place to counterattack and encircle them. Really, the only place France wasn't a tankproof steel fortress was a small strip of land in southeast Belgium known as the Ardennes Forest, and only because the woods were so incredibly dense that there was no way in heck you could drive a tank through there.

So, naturally, that's exactly what the Germans did.

On the morning of May 5, 1940, Germany rolled seven full-strength panzer divisions (each with about three hundred tanks) straight through the Ardennes Forest and out into the open countryside of eastern France. As German Stuka dive-bombers tore down from the sky and mashed up British and French artillery positions, Heinz Guderian and his Nineteenth Panzer Corps hauled forward at full speed, straight past smoking husks of burned-out French trucks and tanks. Blowing through the countryside, Guderian didn't worry about the French positions on his flank, didn't wait for his own infantry (ground soldiers), didn't do anything other than step on the gas and shoot at anything he deemed a threat. Despite his high rank, Guderian himself constantly worked on the front lines of the

battlefield, driving around in a car with a radio so he could be in touch with his men.

All along the rest of the battle lines, the Germans attacked. Tons of paratroopers landed in Belgium and Holland, secured bridges, and captured key government and military objectives. Along the Maginot Line there were also some attacks, but these were only designed to keep France occupied while Guderian's panzers rolled along behind their lines. The German tanks quickly turned back a couple of brave but useless counterattacks by French tanks under a colonel named Charles de Gaulle, then blasted apart a British tank force outside the town of Arras. With their opposition thoroughly demolished, the Germans drove all the way to the coast of France and started rolling up on the now-retreating Allied forces.

Guderian very nearly destroyed the entire British Expeditionary Force, but a heroic defense by the French Army allowed the Brits to reach the port city of Dunkirk and get their guys out of there. The retreat was so desperate that Britain commandeered everything from civilian fishing boats to luxury yachts to wooden sailing ships in order to ferry nearly 340,000 British and French troops back across the English Channel, all while constantly being dive-bombed by German Stuka bombers and strafed by fighter aircraft.

Britain managed to save its army at Dunkirk, but it was pretty much all over for France by this point. Guderian and

A Panzer III in Poland, 1939

the panzers turned south and began their occupation of Paris on June 14, 1940. On the twenty-second, Hitler forced the French government to sign an unconditional surrender in the same train car where Germany had surrendered after World War I. Then he blew up the stone monument commemorating the surrender. Apparently he was still pretty bitter about the whole World War I thing.

In under six weeks, France had suffered 300,000 casualties, compared with just 156,000 German casualties. Over 1.9 million Allied troops surrendered. France was out of the war, Britain was licking its wounds across the Channel, and the United States was still considered a neutral power. Just

German soldiers marching under the Arc de Triomphe in Paris, 1940

like that, Adolf Hitler and Nazi Germany ruled a European empire that stretched from the Pyrenees mountains to the Ukrainian border.

MOLOTOV-RIBBENTROP

Even though the Soviet Union and Nazi Germany hated each other's guts and believed in completely opposite political ideologies, one thing these archenemies could agree on was that they should destroy Poland and a couple of other Eastern European countries and carve everything up between themselves. So, in 1939, the foreign ministers of the two countries secretly signed the Molotov-Ribbentrop Pact. The pact basically said which dictator could conquer which countries—Hitler could have Lithuania, but Stalin wanted Finland and Latvia, and they could divide Poland evenly. The pact also called for ten years of peace between the two countries, even though each dictator knew the other one was crossing his fingers behind his back when he signed it. The "ten years of nonaggression" thing lasted less than two years.

NAZI SYMBOLISM

In case you ever watch all those scary clips of Hitler screaming and yelling and wonder what the heck everyone's talking about, the Nazi Party catchphrase *Sieg heil* means "Hail to victory." The swastika, the hooked cross that appears on Nazi flags, is an ancient Indian symbol representing luck and eternity. It was adopted by Hitler to represent the "pure Aryan race" because he believed the Aryan race originated in northern India.

THE PANZER IV

The only German tank produced throughout World War II was the ever-present Panzer Mark IV tank. Measuring twenty-three feet in length and weighing in at twenty tons, this medium tank had an 11.9-liter V-12 engine that generated three hundred horsepower and could haul along at twenty-six miles per hour. It was equipped with a 75mm main gun and two 7.92mm MG34 machine guns (one in the hull and one in the turret) and rocked 50mm frontal armor to deflect incoming shells and bazooka rounds. It was operated by a crew of five: a driver, a radioman, a loader, a gunner, and the tank commander.

EBEN-EMAEL

The center of the defenses in Belgium was an intimidating stone and steel fortress known as Eben-Emael. Dubbed "the most secure fortress in the world," this structure had 196-foot-tall walls; it housed over twelve hundred defenders, was completely airtight to protect it from gas attacks, and was packed with all kinds of artillery and machine guns. But on the first day of the German attack, an elite group of seventy German commandos silently landed gliders on the roof of the building, infiltrated the upper floors, dropped a bunch of explosives into the interior ventilation shafts, and started clearing out the hallways. The fortress surrendered shortly after. The Germans lost only six men in the entire battle.

KNOW YOUR VEHICLES

	Panzer Mark III	Char D1
TYPE	Medium tank	Heavy tank
COUNTRY	Germany	France
FIRST PRODUCED	1939	1932
LENGTH	20 feet	19 feet
WEIGHT	25 tons	15 tons
ARMOR	30 millimeters	40 millimeters
ENGINE	296-hp Maybach HL120	74-hp Renault V-4
TOP SPEED	25 mph	12 mph
CREW	5	3
ARMAMENT	One 50mm KwK 38 L/42 cannon Two 7.92mm machine guns	One 47mm SA34 cannon Two 7.5mm machine guns

French tanks at the start of the war were every bit as tough as the German ones. But they were built mostly for standing still and laying down fire with big guns and thick armor, and they didn't have the speed to catch up to the German blitzkrieg.

3

THEIR FINEST HOUR

Battle of Britain Day

Southeast England
September 15, 1940

The odds were great; our margins small; the stakes infinite.

—Winston Churchill

PRIME MINISTER WINSTON CHURCHILL WASN'T expecting to witness the biggest day in modern British military history when he and his wife made an unannounced visit to the secret headquarters of Number Eleven Group, Royal Air Force, in the West London neighborhood of Uxbridge on the morning of September 15, 1940. Descending a concrete staircase to a secret James Bond villain–style bombproof bunker sixty feet underground, Churchill was really just expecting to check in on how things were going with the Fighter Command group responsible for defending London's airspace from enemy attacks. You know, chill out, chomp on a cigar or two, and see how things were going. Maybe get a doughnut or something.

It had been six weeks since Adolf Hitler began his relentless aerial bombings designed to blast the British Isles into charcoal. The Nazi Führer had really, really hoped Churchill would just give up after getting his butt whupped in France. But when those pesky Brits simply refused to surrender, Hitler made it his personal mission to sail across the English Channel and hang an obscenely big custom-made Nazi flag down the side of whatever remained of the Big Ben clock tower.

Germany massively outnumbered the British in terms of men and tanks. But their main obstacle to marching over the rubble of London was that there was a really big body of water (the English Channel) between Occupied France and the English countryside, and Hitler's only means of moving large numbers of troops across was on a bunch of unarmed transport barges. To launch any meaningful invasion of England, Hitler would have to annihilate the British Royal Air Force (known as the RAF) so the Brits couldn't just shoot up all his barges full of guys before they got across the water.

It was the Royal Air Force's job to make sure that the Germans never set foot in England.

It wasn't easy. The German Luftwaffe was relentless and powerful and monstrously outnumbered the RAF. The Luftwaffe was under the command of Reichsmarschall Hermann Göring, an extremely successful World War I fighter pilot who was the founder of the German secret police (the Gestapo) and also the chief ranger of all forests in Germany, for some reason. Göring had twenty-five hundred ultramodern fighter planes and heavy bombers, all crewed by veteran pilots with tons of combat experience. In just six weeks they'd launched over seventy daylight raids across England, ruthlessly blasting apart RAF air bases, radar stations, and aircraft-production factories, never giving the defenders a moment to breathe. Just one week before Winston Churchill's unannounced visit to the RAF bunker in West London, on September 7, the Nazis upped their game and started dropping bombs on London itself—not because it had military value but just because they wanted to stomp on Britain's spirit.

Beneath the observation gallery of the bunker sat a big oval table. On it was a map of England, with a bunch of little pieces indicating current positions of British and German aircraft; the pieces could be moved around like in a board game. But instead of Risk, this was real-life people getting blown up by machine-gun fire. Behind the table, a blackboard listed all available fighter squadrons along with their current status. The bunker was manned by a couple dozen women from the Women's Auxiliary Air Force (WAAF) who received radio calls from WAAFs at other air stations. They then used that info to contact RAF fighter squadron bases and to coordinate hundreds of vehicles flying through the skies at three hundred miles per hour with nothing less than the fate of Western democracy in their hands.

When Air Vice Marshal Keith Park greeted Churchill in the bunker around nine AM on the fifteenth, there wasn't much going on. WAAFs were tracking a few German

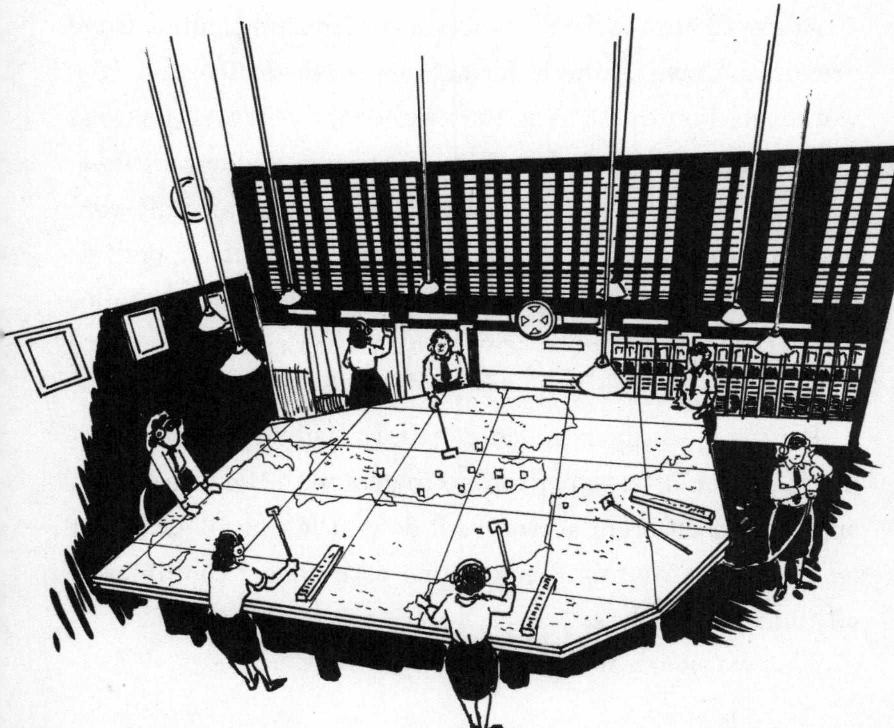

reconnaissance (information-gathering) flights, but the activity really hadn't gotten started yet. Park was a no-nonsense fighter ace from New Zealand who had shot down twenty German planes during World War I. As commander of Number Eleven Group, he had the job of defending London from Luftwaffe bombing raids and hitting the enemy as they crossed the English Channel. Considering that he had only twenty-five squadrons under his command (each squadron was supposed to have twelve aircraft, but this was pretty much impossible to maintain during the war), he was doing a mind-blowingly good job of it.

At eleven AM, the first contacts started coming online. Huge groups of them. Multiple formations marked *40+* and *80+* were placed on the map as the women of the WAAF received more and more reports from WAAFs at radar stations all along the coast. Altogether, nearly a thousand German aircraft were headed straight across the Channel for London itself, endless swarms of enemy fighters and bombers stretched out for miles across the water, all converging to blast the British capital into a crater.

Park moved about quickly, calmly issuing orders, sending squadron after squadron up to deal with the attack as it approached different sectors. All down the line, WAAFs got on the phone, dialing ready rooms with enemy coordinates, altitudes, and orders.

This was going to be big.

Sirens shrieked out across tarmacs at Fighter Command bases across England. Officers yelled for pilots to "scramble" to their aircraft, and in a heartbeat the once-quiet, grassy airfields churned to life. Ground crews raced to their posts to perform final checks on fuel and ammunition, start up the engines, and prepare the strip for takeoff. Pilots in the ready room snapped awake from their naps, already wearing their flight suits, and sprinted down the airstrip for their planes. These exhausted men, most of them between the ages of eighteen and twenty-four, had been engaged in two separate battles the day before (and pretty much every day before that). But despite a brutal two months of nonstop battle, there was no time to rest. The entire country depended on them and their ability to smoke Nazis out of the sky like burning, Swastika-emblazoned comets.

It was almost noon when the awe-inspiring cloud of German heavy bombers arrived within sight of downtown London. Hundreds of Heinkel and Dornier heavy bombers, each packing tons of high explosives, flew together in perfect formation. They were supported by a fierce fighter screen of top-of-the-line Messerschmitt Bf-109s (or Me-109s) each rocking deadly machine guns and cannons. The formation had already been hit in a running battle by wave after wave of British Spitfire and Hurricane fighter planes, but Me-109 pilots such as Adolf Galland had managed to keep the British from doing too much damage to the bomber formations.

German bombers over London

Galland, a dude famous for having a custom ashtray built into his Messerschmitt so he could smoke cigars while fighting (even though Hitler had specifically banned smoking in the Luftwaffe), notched his thirty-third air-to-air kill in the process when he dropped a British Hurricane out of the sky. By the end of the year, his kill total would be in the nineties.

With his eyes fixed on the enemy formation, British Wing Commander Douglas Bader ordered his men to slam it full throttle and scream in for the attack. Leading a fierce fifty-six-plane formation dispatched from Number Twelve Group (based farther north in England), Bader's Air Wing was made up of dedicated veteran pilots from Britain, and also included the Canadians of 242 Squadron, the Polish of 302 Squadron, and the Czechs of 301 Squadron. Diving down out of the sun, the Spitfires and Hurricanes barked fire from eight-packs of .303-caliber machine guns, chewing up the German formation and diving into the already insane fray. The moment Bader's men hit, other planes from Number Eleven Group dove in to face the Germans as well.

The air battle over London quickly spiraled out into hundreds of individual dogfights (planes fighting one another at close range) as formations broke apart, fighter planes chased one another all over the sky, and the entire airspace above London was filled with streams of tracer bullets like something out of an old-school arcade game. Machine gunners in the German Dornier and Heinkel bombers fired in every direction as their pilots tried desperately to stay on target for their attack runs. Nimble, lightweight RAF Spitfires barrel-rolled and climbed with amazing agility, trying to outmaneuver and drop behind their cunning German adversaries. British Hawker Hurricanes wracked German bombers with bullets and then dove down before the Messerschmitts could line them up in their sights.

Hundreds of men were strapped into ultrapowerful metal aircraft five miles above the earth, swirling through the skies

in freezing cold cockpits at three hundred miles per hour, trying to close to within two hundred yards of their rivals so they could get a clear shot. With no power steering, no pressurized cockpits, and no onboard radar to help them out, pilots had to rely solely on their strength, reflexes, and vision to keep them alive and to destroy their enemies.

You know those white lines you sometimes see trailing behind high-flying airplanes? Well, on this day the citizens of London were staring up at hundreds of them swirling in every direction as the battle raged far above. One German bomber, anxious to release his payload, dropped a bomb on the Queen's apartments in Buckingham Palace (she wasn't there at the time). Another bomber nailed the Strand, a big-time shopping district in London. Yet another was shot down and crashed into Victoria train station. One German pilot parachuted down near London's most famous cricket stadium and was grabbed by the people in the stands. A German aircrew that had replaced the tail machine gun on their Dornier with an awesome flamethrower tried to use it, but at the super-high altitude the flame didn't ignite. Instead of belching fire, it just launched oil all over a Spitfire's cockpit and got shot down in return.

In the middle of the fighting, Douglas Bader yanked the control stick of his Hawker Hurricane hard as he dove toward a Dornier bomber. A highly accomplished stunt pilot and an extreme daredevil, Bader had been discharged from the RAF after a nasty wreck in 1931 when he crashed his plane trying

Douglas Bader with his Hawker Hurricane, 1940

to do a low-altitude barrel roll and lost both of his legs. Now he was performing complicated maneuvers with two metal prosthetic legs. After pulling out of his roll, the wing commander unleashed a 9,600-round-per-minute burst of gunfire that ripped off the back end of the Dornier, sending it careening toward the river Thames in flames.

After intense fighting, the German attack was repelled, and the British squadrons landed to rapidly refuel, reload their guns, and patch up minor repairs. No sooner did they touch down than Fighter Command started getting pinged by an entirely new set of radar contacts. Another wave of Germans was headed across the Channel!

And this one was even bigger than the first!

His eyes fixed on the ready board in the command center, Winston Churchill leaned over to Sir Keith Park and quietly asked, "What reserves have we?" Park matter-of-factly responded, "We have none."

Moving at a superhuman NASCAR pit crew–style pace, RAF ground crews worked their magic, even as Luftwaffe bombs blasted the airfields around them. The main enemy force arrived over Kent, on the southeast tip of England, just two hours after the fighting around London had ended.

There were a miraculous eleven Fighter Command squadrons there to meet them.

Among the first to slam headlong into the almost endless wave of Germans were five Hawker Hurricanes of 303 Squadron. The squadron leader, Witold Urbanowicz, had been the instructor at the Polish Air Force College when the Germans attacked in 1939. In the chaos of the blitzkrieg, Urbanowicz evacuated his school, fled across the countryside with a bunch of eighteen-year-old cadets, got them to safety in Romania, then went *back* and fought on the ground as an infantryman. He was captured by the Soviet Union, escaped, went back to Romania, got his cadets, then fled to France. He was evacuated at Dunkirk and swore vengeance. Now he commanded 303 Squadron, a unit of Polish expatriates (expatriates are people who live outside their native country) and by far the unit with the most air-to-air kills in the Battle of Britain. Just a week earlier, Urbanowicz had taken twelve of his boys up against nearly 150 enemy craft and managed to take out eighteen without losing a single pilot. Now he was hoping for the same magic.

Urbanowicz and his Poles flew straight into the German bombers, ignoring the German fighter planes and strafing the bigger craft with everything they had. Urbanowicz himself blasted two Dorniers out of the sky, then led his men down into cloud cover as rage-filled Me-109s descended from above, raking the Hurricanes with machine-gun fire. One of the 303 Squadron planes was hit hard, forcing the pilot to bail out, but as the rest of the Germans were picking out targets, they came face-to-face with ten more squadrons of desperate RAF pilots with nothing to lose, flying at them from above, below, and every other direction. Fighting desperately for their home and their families, the British Royal Air Force swarmed and weaved through the Luftwaffe formations. They smashed the Luftwaffe across a battlefield that ranged eighty miles across England and ultimately drove the Germans back over the Channel. The attack would cost the Luftwaffe sixty aircraft, while the British would lose just twenty-six.

Hitler canceled the planned invasion of England the next day.

The gratitude of every home in our Island, in our Empire, and indeed throughout the world, except in the abodes of the guilty, goes out to the British airmen who, undaunted by odds, unwearied in their constant challenge and mortal danger, are turning the tide of the World War by their prowess and by their devotion. Never in the field of human conflict was so much owed by so many to so few.

—Winston Churchill

FLEEING ON REPLACEMENT LEGS

Douglas Bader became one of Britain's most famous flying aces. He eventually collided with a wrecked Me-109 midbattle and was captured by the Germans. Bader's prosthetic legs were damaged, so he got special permission to have replacement ones flown into Germany by the Red Cross. Then he somehow escaped from the prison camp at Stalag Luft III. He was later recaptured and moved to a different place, and tried to escape from there as well. The Germans finally got sick of this dude running for it, so they locked him up in a super-huge castle until the end of the war.

303 SQUADRON

Urbanowicz's 303 Squadron was engaged for forty-three days during the air war, destroyed 126 enemy aircraft, and lost just five pilots. That was by far the best service record for any squadron in the RAF. After the Battle of Britain, Urbanowicz worked as a combat tactics instructor before quitting the RAF, joining the Flying Tigers (check out chapter 7 for more about these guys), and shooting down two Japanese fighters over China, giving him seventeen kills for the war. Nowadays his story is required reading in Polish grade schools.

THE BATTLE OF THE ATLANTIC

Machines weren't just exploding into flaming wreckage in the skies above England during this time. They were also blowing up in the waters around it.

Great Britain had the best and most powerful surface fleet in Europe, but the Germans counterpunched this by building a fairly scary fleet of over a thousand torpedo-ripping submarines known as U-boats (short for *unterseeboot*, which literally means "undersea boat") that would uppercut the British from beneath the waves. Their primary targets were the large convoys of Canadian transport ships that were bringing US-made supplies and weapons across the Atlantic to England.

Submarine warfare dates back to the days of the CSS *Hunley* accidentally blowing itself up during the American Civil War, but by 1941 tactics and technology had become decidedly deadlier than just sneaking up on a warship and trying to poke it with a mine. Working together in a tactic known as the "wolf pack," German subs like infamous Captain "Silent Otto" Kretschmer's U-99 would typically approach large merchant convoys at night, rise near the surface, rip off a couple of torpedoes, then tear out of there before attack destroyers could swing in with depth charges (underwater bombs). Kretschmer's U-99 accounted for forty-seven kills between 1939 and 1941, making him one of the toughest U-boat aces of the war. The U-boat service in general was responsible for the sinking of 875 Allied ships during 1941 alone.

The back-and-forth sea duels between Nazi subs and Allied convoys went on for the duration of World War II. The Allies lost three thousand ships during the entire naval campaign (sometimes called the "Battle of the Atlantic"), including three aircraft carriers and two battleships, plus nearly fourteen million tons of ammunition, food, supplies, and other vital war equipment. The Germans lost 783 of their 1,162 U-boats by the time the war was over.

KNOW YOUR VEHICLES

	Supermarine Spitfire Mark I	Messerschmitt Bf-109E-3
TYPE	Air superiority fighter aircraft	Air superiority fighter aircraft
COUNTRY	Great Britain	Germany
FIRST PRODUCED	1938	1939
LENGTH	29 feet, 11 inches	28 feet, 4 inches
WEIGHT	5,784 pounds	5,875 pounds
ENGINE	1,030-hp Rolls-Royce Merlin III	1,175-hp Daimler-Benz DB601A
TOP SPEED	355 mph	348 mph
RATE OF CLIMB	2,530 feet per minute	3,200 feet per minute
CREW	1 pilot	1 pilot
ARMAMENT	Eight .303-caliber machine guns	Two 20mm cannons Two 7.92mm machine guns

The Spitfire was more nimble and could make tighter turns than the Messerschmitt. But the German planes could climb and dive more quickly than their British adversaries, making for some epic duels high above the streets of London.

4

OPERATION BARBAROSSA

The German Invasion of Russia

June 22–December 5, 1941
Soviet Union

We have only to kick in the door and the whole rotten structure will come crashing down.

—Adolf Hitler

ONCE IT BECAME APPARENT THAT ADOLF HITLER wasn't going to be able to lunge across the English Channel and park a panzer on the lawn of Buckingham Palace, he turned his attention elsewhere. Namely, he decided to double-cross Josef Stalin, go against the "Hey, I promise not to kill you" nonaggression pact he'd signed a few years earlier with the Russians, and focus the full might of the Nazi war machine right at the heart of the Soviet Union. In a near-perfect display of hardcore backstabbing, on June 22, 1941, Hitler launched 3.8 million men and four thousand tanks into Russia at maximum speed. It would be the largest invasion in the history of warfare.

If you look at the two countries on a map, it might not make a lot of sense for Germany to attack such a large nation, but basically it amounts to this: Hitler hated Russia, Stalin, and all things Communist, and he knew that now was the best chance he'd ever have to kick the butts of all three with one mighty jackbooted swing. Germany was at the height of its power and had just carved through Poland and France like a chain saw through a milk carton. Russia had lost a war to tiny little Finland (although they would take revenge a couple of years later), and Josef Stalin stupidly had two-thirds of his general staff murdered in 1936 because he was paranoid that they didn't like him and were saying mean things behind his back. There would never be a better opportunity, and it was time to strike while the panzer engines were still hot.

Arranged in three army groups, Hitler's tanks rolled out to purge Europe of the Russians; the German crews knew they needed to destroy their enemy quickly before the Russians could get their act together and mount some kind of resistance.

The Russians apparently didn't get the memo that you couldn't really trust this Hitler guy, because they were completely unprepared to have a ridiculously large number of

Germans stomping all over their country. The treads of panzer tanks crushed flower beds and rolled over houses left and right, covering fifty miles in the first two days of the attack and blasting everything in their way. Luftwaffe bombers and aircraft smashed communications, railroads, and enemy positions whenever they felt like it, and there was nothing the Russians could do to stop them.

The Germans used sweeping "pincer" attacks to wrap themselves around the Russian armies and close in like a big, armor-plated lobster claw or that thing you use to try to grab stuffed animals out of vending machines. Basically, tanks would attack head-on from the west while other tanks drove around to the north and south to surround the Russians in a Hot Pocket. That would leave the trapped Russians with two options: surrender or be shot in the front, back, and sides at the same time. At Minsk, in the present-day republic of Belarus, three hundred thousand Russians were forced to surrender when our friend Heinz Guderian surrounded them. Down the road at Smolensk, another three hundred thousand surrendered. Russian divisions were disintegrating all across the front.

Just a month or so into the campaign (known by the German code name Operation Barbarossa), the invincible German Army had won every single battle they'd fought, driven two-thirds of the way to Moscow (the capital of Russia), annihilated a half dozen Russian armies, and captured over a million Soviet soldiers. To put this in perspective, the best guess for total casualty numbers in the *entire* American Civil War was 1.2 million. And that's both armies. *Combined.* Heck, if we want to do a full Guts & Glory series tie-in, the Great Heathen Army of the Vikings was made up of just a couple thousand guys. The Russians were losing at least that many men *every single day for two months straight.*

By the end of July, the road was wide open to Moscow, and things weren't looking good for Uncle Joe Stalin. The German Army was 210 miles away and had twice as many guys as the folks defending the Russian capital, and the Luftwaffe would have clear skies to bomb everything in sight for another two months. In the north, Leningrad (present-day St. Petersburg) was completely surrounded and under siege. In the south, two Russian armies were still clinging to Kiev (in present-day Ukraine), but they were being forced back farther and farther every day.

At this point, Hitler made the sort of tactical error that military historians love to complain and debate about endlessly. Instead of just driving into Moscow and leveling it, he ordered Heinz Guderian to drive south and help out the German forces in Ukraine. Guderian begged and pleaded for Hitler to let him demolish Moscow, but in the end he knew there was no real point in trying to win an argument with Adolf Hitler. He headed south and successfully captured 665,000 Russian troops around Kiev, but by the time he got back to Smolensk it was already the end of September and the horrific Russian winter was starting to roll in.

Before we go any further, let's talk a little bit about the role of the Russian winter in previous wars. In 1707 the eccentric Swedish king Charles XII marched a previously invincible army into Russia to fight Tsar Peter the Great. Charles lost a quarter million men, barely escaped with his life, was stripped of his throne, and spent the next five years hiding in exile. In 1812 French conqueror Napoleon Bonaparte marched his mighty Grande Armée toward Moscow, and Napoleon—a man believed to be one of the world's greatest military geniuses—ended up watching a force of 685,000 French soldiers disintegrate before his very eyes.

Stalin grabbed some popcorn and got pretty pumped up about seeing Hitler suffer a similar fate.

The Russians have a word to describe their rainy season: *rasputitsa*. The translation is a little wonky, but it basically means "all roads disappear." Starting in October, torrential downpours turn the entire countryside into a slimy brown sludge that sort of resembles a chocolate ice-cream sundae with way too much hot fudge on it. The dirt roads that crisscross the land get soaked day and night until they're basically just brown rivers of quicksand. Then, after about a month and a half of people slogging through waist-deep mud so hellacious it sucks horses down to their shoulders and buries the treads of tanks, the rain turns to snow. And winter in Russia is really, *really* cold. So cold that metal moving parts on guns, airplanes, and tanks freeze solid and stop working the way they're supposed to.

Stalin knew all this, and despite having had most of his top generals whacked a few years earlier, he had one man he could count on: Marshal Georgy Konstantinovich Zhukov. Born in 1896 to a peasant family outside Moscow, by 1941 Zhukov was a battle-hardened warrior. Commanding a frontline cavalry unit during World War I, he led his men on daring charges against the Germans on countless occasions. He was wounded severely in that war but recovered in time to serve in the Russian Civil War, where he received the Order of the Red Banner, the first (and highest) military award offered by the Soviet Union. Zhukov had spent the first part of World War II battling the Japanese in Mongolia and was declared "Hero of the Soviet Union" after an epic mission in which he launched a brilliant counterattack that encircled and destroyed an entire Japanese division. Now the fate of Moscow—and all of Mother Russia—was in his hands.

Zhukov was outnumbered and backed up against a wall. The German Wehrmacht was a mere nineteen miles from downtown Moscow and moving in. They were so close that some German troops later claimed they could see the gold domes of the Kremlin, the center of the Soviet government. Realizing that his forces were massively depleted and

demoralized, Marshal Zhukov mobilized the entire city of Moscow for war. Women and girls came out every day to dig a triple ring of antitank pits and trenches. Auto mechanics were called to repair tanks and armored cars. Civilians grabbed rifles and were thrown into battle. All the while, both Russians and Germans struggled through temperatures as cold as minus twenty degrees Fahrenheit, so miserably frigid that machine guns wouldn't fire and aircraft couldn't take off. The subzero temperatures froze the German attack into an armor-plated ice cube, which was such a relief to the Russians defending their homes that they started calling the temperature "General Winter," as if the atmosphere itself were a member of their military.

Every day that the Germans failed to take Moscow was a bonus to Zhukov and the Russians holding the city. Realizing that the situation with the Japanese out in Mongolia wasn't as serious as Stalin expected, Zhukov started bringing in fresh troops along the Trans-Siberian Railway, somehow shuttling thirty full-strength divisions of new soldiers from eastern Russia right into the Moscow train station. The Germans, meanwhile, were dealing with a big-time guerrilla warfare problem, as regular Soviet citizens from areas that had already been conquered by the Nazis were now grabbing weapons and battling the invaders. Trains containing vital supplies needed for the war, like cold-weather clothing (hundreds of thousands of Germans suffered from frostbite because they didn't bring their winter coats when they invaded the USSR in June) and bullets, weren't getting to the front lines because these average Joes (average Ivans?) were ripping up train tracks and bombing railcars. Meanwhile, every German attempt to break through the ring of Russian defenses was violently thrown back, greatly increasing the need for more gear and reinforcements.

By December 5, 1941, the tides of war had turned against Adolf Hitler. The Russian army, now completely reinforced and mega–pumped up by their ability to defend their homeland, bolted out of their trenches and raced through knee-deep snow alongside waves of brand-spanking-new T-34 battle tanks and heavy artillery guns. The German Army, already bummed out and totally not expecting a swarming counterattack in the dead of winter, fell back and withdrew to better positions away from Moscow.

The invincible German blitzkrieg had been stopped less than twenty miles from ultimate victory.

Here they found real war,
but they were not ready for it.

—Marshal Georgy Zhukov, Red Army Chief of Staff

THE COST OF WAR

In the first six months of Operation Barbarossa, over two million Russian soldiers were killed, wounded, or captured. This is enough people to fill every single NFL football stadium in the United States to maximum capacity at the same time.

THE PARTISANS

When Hitler's soldiers marched on some of these Russian cities, particularly the ones in Ukraine, the civilian population brought them flowers and cheered their arrival. Many of these average folks were thinking maybe they'd have a better life under the Nazis than they did under the Soviets. Unfortunately for them, Hitler didn't want anything to do with these people, simply because they weren't German. Death squads known as *Einsatzgruppen* ("deployment groups") murdered tens (if not hundreds) of thousands of innocent civilians. But this ruthless brutality would be Hitler's undoing—these same people who had once greeted him with open arms quickly became rebel guerrilla fighters. Their relentless hit-and-run attacks on the German transportation lines kept Nazi troops outside Moscow from getting adequate supplies of bullets and warm clothing, contributing to their defeat.

HEAVY GUSTAV

To support Operation Barbarossa, the Germans produced some ridiculously huge cannons and artillery pieces. The most famous of these was the awesomely named Heavy Gustav, a four-story-tall gun so humongous that it had to be mounted on a train car. Gustav's 106-foot barrel was about as long as two and a half city buses and was so big you could climb inside it. The gun weighed 1,344 *tons*, could launch an explosive shell the size of a U-Haul over thirty miles, and took a crew of 250 guys to operate.

DEFINITION-ISM

You'll find that most half-decent World War II histories are seasoned with a ton of big, annoying words that all end in the suffix *–ism*. This gets mega-confusing because most of these words aren't the sort of vocab you'd see on a menu at a McDonald's drive-through. Plus, a lot of them have really complicated definitions that aren't easy to understand right away. I'm not going to put you to sleep with all the boring details, but since a heck of a lot of people in this book fought and died horrific deaths because of their beliefs, it's probably important for you to have a general idea of what those beliefs actually were.

Capitalism

Capitalism is an economic system that says people should be able to own their own businesses, and those businesses should be able to do whatever they want. You want to carve logs into cute wooden bunnies and sell them online for ten bucks? Sure, go for it, kid; knock yourself out. You want to buy a bunch of big cargo ships, hire employees, and start a company that ships wooden bunnies to Hong Kong? Of course you can. It's your business, your money, and your life. Do whatever you want.

This makes pretty decent sense, but there are varying degrees of capitalism, and a truly *free-market capitalist* society can get complicated quickly. What if you decide you don't want to sell your bunnies to people with red hair? Sure, it's not fair to redheads, but it's your business, so what's the problem? Now, what if instead of bunnies you make a drug that cures cancer? Can you still exclude part of the population, or is it the government's job to force you to include everyone? What if you have a cure for cancer but decide you want to charge a million dollars a pill for it? As the business owner, you have that right, but is it also the government's job to make life fair for its people? These are all questions that capitalists run into pretty regularly.

Communism

In 1848 a German dude named Karl Marx looked at the capitalist system and decided it was total crap. Marx thought that a capitalist society rewarded business owners for ripping people off and that it gave a bunch of rich jerks control over everything while poor people were basically stuck being slaves to their paychecks forever. His solution was called communism—a system in which individual people own nothing and all the businesses are in the hands of the government. The government controls everything from gas stations to electric companies and gives out equal shares to everybody. You and your neighbor each get the same amount of money for groceries, live in pretty similar houses, and drive similarly priced cars. A doctor is paid the same as an auto mechanic, and while you don't have super-rich people in your country anymore, you don't have super-poor people, either.

This concept sounded pretty darn good to the millions of starving peasants and workers in Russia in the early twentieth century. So in 1917 they overthrew the tsar (basically a king), killed his entire family, and established a communist government set on improving the lives of the regular people. Unfortunately, the problem with communism (sometimes called Marxism or bolshevism) is that some people don't like giving up power, wealth, or fame so someone else can have a little. Think of it this way: If you were a high-ranking government official, would you want to drive the same basic car to work as the guy who comes by on Tuesdays to wash the windows? Or would you maybe try to tweak the paperwork so you get a Ferrari instead?

Communism didn't really play out in the Soviet Union the way Marx had intended, and by the start of World War II, the Soviet Union was firmly in the iron grip of one man: Josef Stalin, the head of the Soviet Communist Party. This guy was in charge of the government, and the government was technically in charge of everything from the candy-bar factory to the military. And disagreeing with Stalin meant you got shipped to a prison camp in Siberia. Talk about a concept backfiring on you.

Democracy

I guess this technically isn't an *–ism*, but we should talk about it anyway. Unlike the first two *–ism*s, democracy has absolutely nothing to do with economics. This is a purely political system where the regular folks in a country get to have a say in what the country does. That probably doesn't seem like a big deal, since it's pretty common these days, but try going back in time to the Dark Ages and telling some sword-swinging king that he should let his peasants vote on whether or not he should still be the king. If you walked out of that meeting with your head attached to your shoulders, I'd be impressed.

Back when the ancient Greeks of Athens invented democracy around 400 BC, it literally meant that every man (yes, just the men—sorry, ladies) in the city came out and voted for things. And whatever got the most votes was what the city did. Nowadays, we have what's called *representative democracy*. This means that we vote for representatives—congressmen and congresswomen, or senators, or members of Parliament—and those people do our voting for us, mostly because we have better things to do than spend all day voting about whether or not to build a new stadium downtown or to increase the sales tax by 1 percent or whatever. Even though these elected people don't always do *exactly* what each voter wants, most folks in a democracy can sleep pretty well knowing that their government's decisions should reflect the voice of the people. As a general rule, when the people of a country get to vote for stuff (and there is more than one option on the ballot!), it's a democracy.

Totalitarianism

Totalitarianism is the opposite of democracy. In this political system, all-consuming power over the government is held by one person or one group of people. Those in authority do whatever they want, regardless of what the citizens think. If it's just one person, like a king or an emperor or a president for life, it's a *dictatorship*. If it's a group of people, it's called an *oligarchy*. If complete power is held by a religious figure or organization, like a high priest or a church, it's called a *theocracy*.

There can be some advantages to this. If you have one guy in charge of everything, he can make decisions and get things done a lot more quickly than a big group of people who have to vote on things and hold elections and all that. Some people think that the best form of government is a *benevolent dictatorship*—a situation where one super-chill dude runs the country, making decisions on his own for the benefit of all his subjects. But how can you be sure the person in power is the right man or woman for the job and has the people's best interests in mind?

Fascism

Fascism is a type of totalitarian dictatorship based on the concept that "only the strong survive" and that the strength of the country is more important than the interests of the people. All power is in the hands of one leader who controls absolutely everything, including (ideally) the minds of the people. A fascist government controls every aspect of the economy, just as a communist government does, but the reasoning behind it is very different. Communists think a society's resources should be owned by the government and all money distributed equally among the citizens. Fascist governments like Nazi Germany and Mussolini's Italy told private business owners exactly what to produce and how to produce it, and the businessmen were happy to do it because it was supposed to be for the good of their country...and because if they didn't, they'd be arrested as traitors and replaced with someone who would. Under fascism, everyone in the society is expected to be completely loyal to the government and opposition is not allowed.

If this sounds kind of like the Soviet Union under Stalin, that's because it is. The primary difference is that Hitler and Stalin had very different outlooks on *why* they should rule the world—Hitler wanted to make the land great for the German people, and Stalin's intention was to free the poor people of the world from oppressive businessmen. But honestly, in practice, these goals looked surprisingly similar.

KNOW YOUR VEHICLES

	Sturmgeschütz (StuG) III	T-26
TYPE	Assault gun	Light tank
COUNTRY	Germany	Soviet Union
FIRST PRODUCED	1940	1931
LENGTH	22 feet, 6 inches	15 feet, 3 inches
WEIGHT	26 tons	10.6 tons
ARMOR	80 millimeters	15 millimeters
ENGINE	296-hp Maybach HL 120 gasoline	90-hp T26 4-cylinder gasoline
TOP SPEED	25 mph	19 mph
CREW	4	3
ARMAMENT	One 75mm StuK 40 L/48 cannon One 7.92mm machine gun	One 45mm 20K cannon One 7.62mm machine gun

The difference between an "assault gun" and a regular tank is that an assault gun like the German StuG III didn't have a turret, so it could only shoot at what was right in front of it. Designed for sniping, ambushes, or straight-ahead attacks, the StuG was way cheaper to make than a regular tank because it didn't have as many moving parts, and it was just as deadly. While the Russians were turning out some state-of-the-art T-34 and KV-1 tanks in 1940, the vast majority of their tanks were T-26 light tanks, which were in over their heads against the German guns.

5

DAY OF INFAMY

The Japanese Attack on the US Pacific Fleet

December 7, 1941
Pearl Harbor, Hawaii

Air raid Pearl Harbor. This is not a drill.

—Loudspeaker announcement,
Naval Station Pearl Harbor

IT WAS JUST ANOTHER BEAUTIFUL DAY IN PARAdise. Pretty girls in bathing suits lay out in the sun on Waikiki Beach, soaking up the morning rays. Surfer dudes caught monster waves on Oahu's North Shore. Couples went for walks on the Honolulu boardwalk, headed out to church, or went swimming in the calm waters of the Pacific. At the US Navy base nearby, sailors slept late to recover from Saturday night's parties or sat down to breakfast with their comrades.

They talked about girls, cars, or sports and listened to the radio playing those chill Hawaiian ukulele jams that make you want to wear a grass skirt and drink a brightly colored drink with a little umbrella sticking out of it. The morning of December 7, 1941, began like any other lazy Sunday for the sailors and airmen of Naval Station Pearl Harbor on the sunny island of Oahu in Hawaii.

It wouldn't end that way.

Two hundred and thirty miles north of Honolulu and the entire United States Navy Pacific Fleet, Admiral Chuichi Nagumo of the Imperial Japanese Navy (IJN) grimly scanned maps on the bridge of his flagship, the mighty aircraft carrier *Akagi*. Nagumo and his fleet had departed from Japan in complete secrecy, crossing the Pacific in just over a week under total radio silence, all the way to the shores of America. Lined up on the decks of six aircraft carriers, Japanese ground crew cheered and waved as hundreds of Japanese fighter and bomber aircraft roared toward their targets.

Back in 1940, the United States had told Japan to stop shooting people in China and Vietnam, and the American government had cut Japan off from vital trade resources like steel and oil. The only way Japan could continue its expansion in Asia was to take these resources by force, whether America liked it or not. So they needed to strike the United States first and break the Americans' will.

Americans were weak. They were soft. They didn't have the

stomach for war. Chuichi Nagumo knew it, and he intended to prove it.

One hundred and eighty-three aircraft in tight formation flew in low across the northern part of Oahu (the Hawaiian island where the capital city, Honolulu, is located). Forward American radar positions registered their approach, but radar techs mistakenly identified them as US B-17 bombers that were expected to arrive from San Francisco at eight AM, and they didn't bother mentioning it to anyone. Skimming over the North Shore, the Japanese made their way over the forested mountains toward their objective. Passing over the last ridge, they saw it: Battleship Row. The entire US Pacific Fleet. Ninety United States Navy vessels, including eight hulking battleships bristling with unmanned gun turrets, all sitting together so perfectly they might as well have had bull's-eyes painted on them.

In the lead Nakajima B5N "Kate" torpedo plane (find more information on plane nicknames at the end of this chapter), Commander Mitsuo Fuchida flicked open a radio channel and gave the command. "*Tora! Tora! Tora!*" came over the speakers of every plane in the formation. *Tora* means "tiger," but in this case, it meant that total surprise had been achieved and to open fire. The call came through so clearly across secure Japanese channels that even Admiral Isoroku Yamamoto heard it while listening in his war room at three o'clock in the morning in Japan.

The bombers dove into the harbor on their attack runs. The first group of B5N Kates went low, scraping the surface of the waves before dropping their torpedoes into the water. In the opening barrage, seven torpedoes struck the battleship USS *West Virginia*, one after the other, rocking the ship with mighty explosions and sending water rushing into the lower decks. Two more torpedoes hit the battleship *Tennessee*. In minutes, another battleship, the *Oklahoma*, was listing, burning, and slipping beneath the waves, taking some of its crew with it.

A separate wave of Kates was packing massive ship-killing bombs, which rained on the fleet with devastating results. One of these, an armor-piercing bomb that weighed 1,760 pounds, roughly the same as a large cow, punched through the forward deck of the battleship *Arizona* and landed in the main ammunition room. Every bullet on the ship ignited at once in a giant, fiery explosion that rocked the entire harbor and blasted the ship apart. Down the line, explosions and fire from burning ships poured black smoke into the sky.

All across the island, American troops were jarred into action by the sounds of the chaos around them. They were caught completely off-guard by the surprise attack. Ammunition crates were locked, guns were unloaded, planes were parked in formation on the runway, and half the base was still asleep. But these brave men weren't about to let the Japanese get out of there without a fight. Aboard the USS *West Virginia*, already burning and sinking, Doris Miller

US battleships burning at Pearl Harbor

raced out to the deck. An African-American ship's cook and former high school football player from Texas, Miller hadn't been trained to work the deck machine gun. But that didn't stop him from slamming a box of .50-caliber bullets into it and opening fire at the swarm of Japanese planes circling above.

With his ship still being rocked by explosions, Miller barked out a constant stream of antiaircraft fire, gritting his teeth as his bullets struck the fuselages of enemy bombers. The ship's

cook manned his position until he'd shot every bullet he had, leaving his post only on the orders of his mortally wounded commanding officer, Captain Mervyn Bennion. Some gunners, like Machinist's Mate Robert Scott, held their posts to the bitter end. Scott was a gunner aboard the battleship USS *California* and kept his AA (antiaircraft) guns ripping even after torpedoes tore a hole in the ship's hull, blew up the antiaircraft ammo storage room, and started filling the room with rushing water. He went down with the ship.

At the end of Battleship Row, just beyond the smoking hulk of the *Arizona*, the USS *Nevada* somehow got its boilers up and running and prepared to make a run for it out of the kill zone. The chief boatswain, Edwin J. Hill, bravely ran to the dock and single-handedly untied the *Nevada* from its moorings while being strafed by machine-gun fire from Japanese Zeros. As the ship was pulling away, this hardcore, ultradevoted sailor stripped off his shirt, ran to the end of the dock, jumped into the water, and swam back to the ship so he could help it fight. The *Nevada* steamed full ahead, running for it, its guns blasting AA fire in every direction, a brief glimmer of hope to all those sailors who saw it on the move.

Elsewhere on the island, a squadron of D3A "Val" dive-bombers screamed down from high altitude and dropped accurate bombs onto the tarmac at Hickam and Wheeler airfields, annihilating American aircraft while they were still parked on the landing strip. Zeros strafed barracks and hangars with machine-gun fire, bombers blew up aircraft left and right, and Army Air Force crews and pilots scrambled in every direction to escape the destruction.

George Welch and Kenneth Taylor, two hard-partying guys who had been out dancing their tails off at nightclubs the evening before, awoke in their barracks and ran to the parking lot. Still wearing their rumpled-up tuxedoes from last night's party, they hopped into Welch's Buick and burned rubber down sixteen miles of winding mountain roads as Zeros zoomed overhead. When they got to the airfield, they jumped out, commandeered two P-40 Warhawk fighter planes without any authorization, and got airborne to fight the Japanese.

As they climbed to combat altitude, they saw a second wave of aircraft coming—another 171 Japanese attack planes diving into the fray.

Welch and Taylor headed straight to a formation of Vals and started lighting them up with their .303-caliber machine guns, breaking them apart and sending enemy aircraft roaring down in flames. In the swirling battle in the skies above Hawaii, these two cagey pilots shot down seven of the twenty-nine Japanese planes destroyed in the fight. Both men had their P-40s shot up, but every time they ran out of bullets, they landed, had aircrews quickly rearm them, and took off right back into the fight. They were both nominated for the Medal of Honor but didn't receive it because their towering acts of heroic bravery took place after they'd received a direct order from a superior officer not to undertake any towering acts of heroic bravery.

The Japanese attack ended as suddenly as it had begun. The raid on Pearl Harbor had lasted just two hours but had caused catastrophic damage to the American fleet. Twenty US ships had been sunk or damaged, including all eight battleships in the harbor, two heavy cruisers, four destroyers, and nine support craft. A total of 188 American planes were destroyed on the ground and another 159 damaged; 2,403 Americans were dead. Another 1,178 were wounded.

The Japanese had lost just twenty-nine aircraft.

Admiral Nagumo had expected the attack to break the American spirit, destroy the navy, and strike fear into the heart of the enemy. It did no such thing. Instead, when Americans heard the emergency bulletins break across their radios later that day, they swore vengeance. At the urging of President Franklin D. Roosevelt, Congress declared war on Japan the very next day. Germany then declared war on the US, and America was now fully involved in World War II.

REBUILDING THE FLEET

Ultimately, the carnage at Pearl Harbor didn't set the American navy back as far as you might think. Pearl was a shallow harbor, meaning that all the battleships except the *Arizona* could be raised, repaired, and sent back into service. The *Nevada*, which was hit badly in the second wave of Japanese attacks, was the first American battleship to fire on enemy positions during D-Day (more on this in chapter 15), and it also participated in the bombardment of Okinawa. Most important, all three US aircraft carriers were out of port that day, saving them from destruction.

DOOLITTLE'S RAID

Just four months after Pearl Harbor, the United States retaliated with a surprise attack of its own. Crossing the Pacific in complete radio silence, an aircraft carrier task force under the command of Lieutenant Colonel Jimmy Doolittle sailed just off the coast of mainland Japan and launched sixteen B-25 Mitchell bombers on a daring daylight bombing raid on Tokyo itself. The B-25 was in no way designed to be launched off an aircraft carrier, but that didn't stop Doolittle from doing it. The bombers pounded the Japanese capital, driving home a message that the United States wasn't going down without a fight.

THE BATTLE OF LOS ANGELES

On a weirder note, a couple of months after Pearl Harbor there was a bizarre incident in Los Angeles when ground control units freaked out because they thought the Japanese were launching an air raid on California. On the night of February 24, 1942, AA units outside LA flipped on high-powered searchlights and started blasting the sky with explosive shells and .50-caliber machine guns, ripping off over fourteen hundred cannon shots and several thousand rounds of machine-gun bullets in the course of an hour. Even though it turned out that the "Battle of Los Angeles" was probably just a bunch of jumpy guys firing at nothing, a lot of crackpot conspiracy theorists like to say that they were actually freaked out by UFOs and trying to shoot down alien spaceships or something. This, however, seems unlikely.

WHAT'S IN A NAME?

Fighter pilots skimming along the water at three hundred miles an hour didn't want to have to scream into their radios things like "Hey, guys, I've got a Mitsubishi A6M3 Navy Type Zero Carrier Fighter Model 32 on my tail—help!" So the Allies came up with nicknames for the various Japanese airplanes. For instance, the Nakajima E2N Navy Type 15 Reconnaissance Floatplane became known as "Bob," which was way easier to remember and didn't require two paragraphs of text to recite the name of a single aircraft. The Allies gave male names to fighters and spy planes, female names to bombers and transports, tree names to training aircraft, and bird names to gliders. Here are some examples:

JAPANESE MILITARY OFFICIAL DESIGNATION	ALLIED REPORTING NAME
Nakajima E8N Navy Type 95 Reconnaissance Seaplane	DAVE
Kokusai Ku-8 Army Type 4 Special Transport Glider	GOOSE
Nakajima B5N Navy Type 97-1 Carrier Attack Bomber	KATE
Kawanishi E15K Navy Type 2 High-Speed Reconaissanse Seaplane	NORM
Nakajima Ki-43 Army Type 1 Fighter	OSCAR
Mitsubishi K3M Navy Type 90 Crew Training Aircraft	PINE
Mitsubishi Ki-21 Army Type 97 Heavy Bomber	SALLY
Tachikawa Ki-9 Army Type 95-1 Intermediate Training Aircraft	SPRUCE
Kawasaki Ki-61 Army Type 3 Fighter	TONY
Aichi D3A Navy Type 99 Dive-Bomber	VAL
Mitsubishi A6M Navy Type 0 Carrier Fighter	ZERO

ANNIE FOX

One of the true unsung heroes of the Pearl Harbor attack was Annie Fox, an army lieutenant assigned to command the hospital at Hickam Field. As wounded and dying men flooded into her infirmary, Lieutenant Fox worked tirelessly to get them treated and healed, despite not having nearly enough staff or facilities. With Japanese planes strafing the field around her and bombing the base less than a mile away, the super-dedicated nurse kept her crews focused, setting up a triage system that utilized everything from the waiting rooms to the hospital's front lawn to make sure she could save as many people as possible. Fox was the first woman to receive the Purple Heart (now the Bronze Star) for a "singularly meritorious act of extraordinary fidelity or essential service."

THE FALL OF SINGAPORE

At the same time the Japanese were nailing Pearl Harbor with a few billion torpedoes and bombs, they were also launching coordinated attacks on US bases in the Philippines and on Wake Island, a tiny island in the Pacific Ocean. Both bases fell within just a few days, with well over a thousand American soldiers forced to surrender to the enemy. Then the Japanese moved on to attack British holdings in Singapore and Malaysia. Racing south through Thailand and Singapore, the Japanese steamrolled all in their path, dismantling British and Indian resistance and punching through defenses that the Brits had once thought were impenetrable.

The Royal Navy sent in the battleship HMS *Prince of Wales* along with a couple of support ships to try to fight off the Japanese landing craft, but the entire force was hammered by Japanese ship-smashing attack planes, and the *Prince of Wales* blew up and sank. Meanwhile, outnumbered but determined Japanese troops charged through the jungles of Southeast Asia and attacked without mercy. The British garrison at Singapore (ninety thousand men in total) surrendered after just four days of fighting when the Japanese snuck up through the jungle and attacked the base from the back. Hong Kong fell in two weeks. Japanese landings in Burma and Rangoon ripped apart defenses, sending any surviving British and Commonwealth (see "The Commonwealth" in chapter 12) forces fleeing into India to regroup. Other Pearl Harbor–style air raids strafed Allied bases in New Guinea and on mainland Australia.

The speed and ferocity of Japan's assault on the Allies was completely unexpected and caught pretty much everyone unaware. It took Imperial Japan just six weeks to lock all of Southeast Asia and the Pacific Islands in an icy death grip.

KNOW YOUR VEHICLES

	Curtiss P-40B Warhawk	Mitsubishi A6M Zero
TYPE	Fighter aircraft	Fighter aircraft
COUNTRY	United States	Japan
FIRST PRODUCED	1941	1940
LENGTH	31 feet, 6 inches	29 feet, 9 inches
WEIGHT	7,326 pounds	5,555 pounds
ENGINE	1,150-hp Allison V-1710-39 V-12	950-hp Nakajima Sakae 12 radial
TOP SPEED	352 mph	331 mph
RATE OF CLIMB	2,860 feet per minute	3,100 feet per minute
CREW	1	1
ARMAMENT	Four .50-caliber machine guns	Two 20mm cannons Two 7.7mm machine guns

Welch, Taylor, and the American "Flying Tigers" (more on them at the end of chapter 7) battling in China flew Curtiss P-40B Warhawks. These were cool-looking fighters that were significantly bigger and heavier than the quick, agile Japanese Zeros. Warhawks could hold their own at high speed, but at slow speeds the nimble Zeros could fly circles around them. Most American pilots chose to fly in at full throttle, open fire, then disengage and circle back around to avoid dogfighting the quick enemy planes.

6

WHO DARES, WINS

Paddy Mayne and the Special Air Service

December 14, 1941–October 28, 1942
North Africa

When you enter a room full of the enemy, kill the first one that moves—he has started to think and is therefore dangerous.

—Major Paddy Mayne, First SAS Regiment

THE STORY OF ROBERT "PADDY" MAYNE READS like something out of a hardcore action movie or the intro to a first-person shooter video game: A gritty, ultratough Royal Commando sits alone in a rat-infested cell in some hellhole in Egypt awaiting a court-martial. The six-foot, four-inch, two-hundred-pound warrior from Northern Ireland is there because he punched out a superior officer and then tried to kill the guy with a bayonet. It was his second arrest in the last year (a few months back he dragged a bartender out of a crowded nightclub and made him "dance" by shooting at the poor chump's feet with a revolver). Now Captain Mayne is staring defiantly ahead, when suddenly a light comes on in the dungeon and a familiar face looms up at the bars. A tall, steel-jawed Scottish aristocrat, Lieutenant Colonel David Stirling, has come with an offer: Sit here and rot or help me lead a small, elite squad of black-ops special forces. We'll be going deep behind enemy lines in the Sahara Desert and wreaking havoc on some of the German Army's most ferocious troops. It's a suicide mission, packed with glory and death mashed together like a bullet sandwich. The best-case scenario has you coming home in a takeout box. But you'll get to kill a lot of Nazis in the process.

I like to imagine Paddy Mayne staring grimly at David Stirling for a full minute, then asking when he can get started.

In the closing weeks of 1941, things were looking bad for the Allies in World War II. Really bad. Hitler's goose-stepping hordes of soldiers stretched from Paris to Moscow, holding all of Europe in a fearsome grip. Now Hitler was beginning to stretch his talons into North Africa as well, thanks to the efforts of Marshal Erwin Johannes Eugen Rommel—a master of blitzkrieg so brilliant and deadly he was known to the British as "the Desert Fox."

Rommel had been called into North Africa after Mussolini's Italians had failed to conquer Libya, and in just a few months the Desert Fox took a demoralized Italian force and turned

it into a world-destroying juggernaut. An old-school soldier who earned Germany's top award for military bravery by storming enemy positions during World War I, Rommel literally wrote the book on fighting with infantry in modern combat. (Seriously, it's called *Infantry Attacks*, and it was read by everyone from Hitler to US general George S. Patton.) Rommel led alpine troops through the mountains during World War I and commanded the Führer's bodyguard unit during the invasion of Poland. His Seventh Panzer Division formed one arm of the pincer that helped Guderian destroy the French Army in the early days of the war. Now in command of the elite German "Afrika Korps," the Desert Fox staged blitzkrieg attacks that routinely outmaneuvered, encircled, and destroyed British forces from Libya to Cairo. By 1942 he'd already put Nazi Germany in an excellent position to seize Egypt, the Suez Canal (a waterway connecting the Red Sea and the Mediterranean Sea), and the oil fields of the Middle East from Great Britain's control. This would be disastrous for the Allies.

And it was up to men like Paddy Mayne and David Stirling to help stop it.

The Afrika Korps seemed unstoppable on the battlefield, but it did have one weakness: its supply lines. With Rommel's troops spread out across North Africa and not many roads to drive on, it was a huge pain to bring necessary food, bullets, bombs, fuel, and reinforcements all the way from Rommel's base in Tripoli to his front lines on the Egyptian border. Stirling decided that if Great Britain couldn't win the war on the front lines, it could sure as heck cut off Rommel's reinforcements. So he formed a unit known simply as "L Detachment" to deal with it. We know it better today as the Special Air Service—the British SAS—one of the world's first special-forces operations. A small team of sixty men were handpicked for their toughness, fighting spirit, and ability to survive in inhuman situations. Climbing hundred-foot sand dunes in the 130-degree heat of the Sahara Desert and braving sandstorms, flash floods, dehydration, and subzero nighttime temperatures, the men of L Detachment were expected to be the best of the best. Their mission was to go in with guns blazing and hammer Nazi airfields, supply dumps, and

Jeep patrol from L Detachment
Special Air Service (SAS) in North Africa, 1943

refueling stations with no hope of reinforcements or rescue, then get the heck out of there before anyone knew what had happened.

To accomplish this superhuman task, the SAS had twenty customized four-wheel-drive jeeps, all tricked out with extra ammo, fuel, bombs, grenades, and spare tires. They were packing twin-linked .303-caliber Vickers machine guns mounted on the passenger side of the vehicle. Their tactics were straightforward and, honestly, completely bonkers: Drive through the Sahara Desert at night; blow past minefields, rocks, wrecked vehicles, and quicksand using nothing but the stars and a compass for direction (Google Maps hadn't been invented yet); then drive the jeeps straight onto the German airstrips and open fire at anything with a swastika painted on it. Pedal to the metal, the SAS would chuck bombs and grenades and fire their machine guns, then peel out leaving nothing but smoking craters and ruins in their wake.

If that sounds awesome and insane, it was.

Paddy Mayne, the second-in-command, quickly earned a reputation for being the most die-hard and fearless man in L Detachment. In the middle of one of his first fights, with German troops scrambling around trying to figure out what was going on, Mayne ran over to an undestroyed Nazi bomber, planted a plastic explosive (a powerful explosive material that

feels a lot like Play-Doh) on it, then calmly walked back to his jeep as the aircraft violently exploded behind him. The entire raid lasted just fifteen minutes, but by the time dawn broke, over thirty German aircraft had been destroyed, a dozen more were damaged, and an antiaircraft gun had been knocked out of action. Just one SAS man had been killed.

In another mission, Mayne drove his jeep up to the barbed wire surrounding a base, crawled underneath it, blew up twenty-four German planes with homemade bombs, then kicked in the door of the German barracks and sprayed it with fire from his submachine gun. Anyone still moving had to deal with Mayne, the hulking former member of the British National Rugby Team and the 1936 Irish Universities'

Heavyweight Boxing champ. After punching out Nazis and flicking the switch on the bomb detonators, Mayne noticed that one Me-109 fighter plane hadn't exploded, so he ran over to the aircraft and pulled the control panel out of the cockpit with his bare hands before running back to his jeep and escaping. Less than a week later he was back at it again, pulling off another wild, gunslinging jeep raid that destroyed twenty-seven Nazi fighters, bombers, and transport planes.

From December 1941 through October 1942, the men of L Detachment successfully pulled off forty daring raids, blowing up everything from fuel depots and ammo dumps to airstrips and communications posts. They've been credited with destroying 320 German aircraft during this period, almost single-handedly crippling the Luftwaffe in North Africa with nothing more than two dozen jeeps and a ton of plastic explosive. Without all those German fighter planes to give them trouble, the British Desert Air Force was able to hammer German trucks and supply planes as they tried to bring desperately needed material to Rommel's front lines.

The Desert Fox resorted to drastic measures, including using captured British trucks and fuel to keep his panzers running, but in the end he simply ran out of gas and ammunition. An estimated two-thirds of the supplies and reinforcements sent to him from Germany were either sunk in the Mediterranean by the Royal Navy, blown up by the Desert Air Force, or trashed by the SAS.

In October 1942, the Germans attempted one more blitz but reached the limit of their supply lines outside the British-controlled city of El Alamein in Egypt. The British commander, Field Marshal Bernard Montgomery, seized the opportunity. He launched a gutsy night attack on the evening of October 28, spearheaded by troops from all across the British Empire—Canadians, Australians, Scots, New Zealanders, South Africans, and Indians all bravely hurled themselves into the fray. Under the cover of an artillery barrage, the Fifty-First Scots Highlanders belted out songs on their bagpipes as British X Corps tanks and infantry from New Zealand and Australia bayonet-stormed through a minefield into Rommel's forces. The Desert Fox, unable to maneuver his blitzkrieg, found himself being hammered on the defensive. It would be the first major battlefield defeat of his career.

Badly bloodied, Rommel's forces limped out of Egypt. Bernard "Monty" Montgomery chased them for three months back to Tripoli. US troops under George S. Patton landed on the west coast of North Africa in early 1943, and the Axis forces in North Africa were squeezed out on both sides. They would surrender a few months later.

As for Paddy Mayne, he ended up taking over command of the newly christened First SAS Regiment after Lieutenant Colonel Stirling was captured during a raid in 1943. Mayne would lead his team on more dangerous raids across Italy, including one time when he and fifty soldiers landed on a beach in the middle of the night, climbed a sheer cliff face with ropes and grappling hooks, attacked an Italian fortress, killed or captured seven hundred guys, blew up their coastal artillery, and drank all their wine. Another time, he mounted machine guns on rubber rafts and captured the town of Termoli, then held it for three days against repeated German counterattacks. Later, in France, he rescued a pinned-down team of Canadian soldiers by kicking out the windshield of a jeep, resting a Bren machine gun on the dash, and driving straight into enemy territory. He controlled the steering wheel with his left hand and shot the gun with his right, piling wounded men up in the back of the jeep whenever he encountered them. How there hasn't been a Jason Statham movie about this guy is beyond me.

After the war, Paddy Mayne, the original founder of the SAS, would retire to a quiet life raising chickens and going on Antarctic expeditions. He was denied the Victoria Cross (Britain's highest military honor) on the grounds of his being a jerk to all his commanding officers, but he remains the only man in the British military to receive the Distinguished Service Order (the second-highest military honor) on four separate occasions.

Lieutenant Colonel Robert Blair "Paddy" Mayne, Special Air Service (SAS), 1942

GET OFF MAH LAWN!

Charles Upham was a New Zealand sheepherder and one of only three men to receive Britain's highest military award, the Victoria Cross, twice. Sent to Crete (the largest of the Greek islands) with the New Zealand Expeditionary Force to fight Hitler in 1941, he was on the receiving end of a massive paratrooper assault and ended up taking out three machine-gun teams with grenades and a pistol. He then held off repeated counterattacks, despite being wounded multiple times by mortars and bullets. After Crete, he redeployed to El Alamein, where he blew up an armored car full of guys with a grenade and led an attack against an Afrika Korps bunker despite taking a bullet through his elbow. He survived the war, went back to New Zealand, and for the rest of his life refused to allow any German-made automobiles on his farm.

ESCAPE TO THE LEGION

Besides facing off with the SAS, Rommel's Afrika Korps also went up against a legendary force of elite desert fighters: the French Foreign Legion. Composed of criminals, tough guys, and other ugly, dirty warrior types, the Legion was a haven for the meanest people on earth because it gave even the most violent criminals in the world an opportunity to wipe their slate clean, take a new identity, and then die gloriously for the honor of France. Surrounded by the blitzkrieg of the city of Bir Hakeim in Libya, the Legionnaires battled like demons despite being outnumbered ten to one by Rommel's Italian troops. Finally, after fifteen days of cutting down repeated attacks, the Legion decided it was time to break out of the encirclement. Leading the charge in the first car was General Marie-Pierre Koenig and his personal driver, a British woman named Susan Travers, who had risen to the rank of sergeant major in the Foreign Legion. In complete darkness, Travers drove like a maniac through a minefield while Nazi bombers strafed the ground around her, leading the way for the Legion to get back to Allied lines. A couple of days later, General Koenig's assistant counted eleven bullet holes in various parts of the car.

ALL-STAR TANK COMMANDER

A one-time member of the South African National Cricket Team, Bob Crisp was a notorious adventurer and ladies' man who made a name for himself first as an all-star bowler (similar to a pitcher in baseball) and then as a Nazi-killing tank commander with the Third Royal Tank Regiment. Commanding an M3 Stuart tank against Germans in Yugoslavia, Crisp destroyed twelve Nazi panzers, shot down a twin-engine Heinkel bomber with a .50-caliber machine gun, was wounded five times, and survived having six tanks shot out from underneath him by the enemy. One time in Africa he jumped into a signal corps tank (despite having no authority to do so) and used it to destroy three Italian antitank cannons. He would be promoted three times in the war, but all three times he'd get busted back down because of "inappropriate behavior," like blowing off his post to go into town and party with cute girls at dance halls.

MAD JACK CHURCHILL

In my opinion, sir, any officer who goes into action without his sword is improperly dressed.

—Lieutenant Colonel Jack Churchill, Royal Marine Commandos

One of the most colorful special-operations warriors of World War II was the ridiculously awesome Colonel Jack Malcolm Thorpe Fleming Churchill. Known as "Mad Jack" Churchill, this fearless, swashbuckling Englishman spent the war performing incredible acts of bravery. He also won major style points for going into every live-fire combat situation carrying a Scottish broadsword, an old-school bow and arrow, and a set of well-worn bagpipes.

Before the war, Churchill (no relation to Winston Churchill) had driven his motorcycle around India and represented Britain in the 1939 World Archery Championship. The training really paid off, because while the Brits were evacuating Dunkirk in 1940, he killed a Nazi with an arrow while executing a raid on a German supply depot—an operation he took on without any authorization. He'd be shot in the neck by a Nazi machine gun a couple of days later, but this didn't stop him from saving the life of a fellow officer, making his way back to

England, and joining up with a brand-new special-forces unit known as the Commandos.

Mad Jack wasn't really sure what a Commando was, but he wanted in, and on his first mission he was ordered to lead a small team of super-jacked secret agents on a stealth raid against a well-defended German coastal fortress in occupied Norway. Moments before the mission began, Jack was blasting "The March of the Cameron Men" on his bagpipes as hard as a human being could possibly pipe it. When the landing ramp hit the water, he raised his shining steel Scottish-style claymore broadsword over his head and charged, screaming "*COMMMMANNNNNNNDOOOOOO!!!!!!!!*"

He captured the fortress in under twenty minutes.

When the Allies invaded Italy in 1943, the guys from Mad Jack's Number Two Commando captured the town of Pigoletti from the Italians by shooting and hollering and throwing so many bombs that the defenders thought they were being attacked by half the British Army. Mad Jack had just fifty men under his command. A hundred and thirty-six Italians surrendered to him.

Then, just to one-up that feat of heroic epicness, Churchill and his aide captured forty-two German prisoners and a mortar team in one night, using only his broadsword. He took a guard as a human shield, went from guard post to guard post, and ordered the men to surrender in such a commanding and charismatic way that they basically just snapped to attention and said "Yes, sir!"

Mad Jack was eventually taken prisoner while fighting alongside Josip Tito's partisans (an anti-Nazi resistance group) in Yugoslavia. Out of bullets for every gun he had (including his pistol!), Jack started playing sad songs on his bagpipes until the Germans threw hand grenades at him to get him to stop. He was taken to a Nazi POW (prisoner of war) camp in September 1944 but immediately dug a tunnel out of there and avoided capture for fourteen days before being brought back in. Shortly after that, he escaped again, this time by jumping out of a moving truck as he was being transported to a different prison.

He ran back to Allied lines, finished out the war, and later received a medal for rescuing doctors, students, and patients from a Jerusalem hospital while the city was under attack at the height of the 1948 Arab-Israeli war. Wearing his full dress military uniform, including his sword, Mad Jack walked right down the middle of the street without even attempting to hide behind cover. The guys who were shooting rockets at the hospital were so confused that they didn't shoot at him!

He also had a small role as an archer in the 1952 movie *Ivanhoe*, then retired to Australia and spent most of the 1950s catching sick half-pipe action on custom surfboards he designed and built himself.

KNOW YOUR VEHICLES

	Willys 5CWT 4x4 Car, L Detachment	Junkers Ju-87B Stuka
TYPE	Modified Willys MB jeep 4x4	Ground attack aircraft/ dive-bomber
COUNTRY	United States (purchased by Great Britain)	Germany
FIRST PRODUCED	1941	1939
LENGTH	11 feet	36 feet, 1 inch
WEIGHT	2,453 pounds	12,880 pounds
ENGINE	54-hp Willys Model MB	1,184-hp Junkers Jumo 211 inverted V-12
TOP SPEED	65 mph	255 mph
CREW	2	2
ARMAMENT	Two .303-caliber machine guns	Two 20mm autocannons; two forward-facing 7.92mm machine guns; one rear-facing 7.92mm machine gun; one 550-pound bomb; four 110-pound bombs

SAS jeeps carried machine guns that were originally supposed to be mounted on planes. These were the only kind of machine gun they could get their hands on, which was perfect, because the SAS needed to shoot at German aircraft. When they assaulted a runway, they could rip apart Stukas and enemy transport and bomber planes on the ground, but once the planes were up in the air, the Germans could easily smash the SAS jeeps to smithereens.

★★★ 7 ★★★

DAUNTLESS

The Battle of Midway

June 4, 1942
Midway Island

My orders were to make a group attack on the enemy striking force. Radio silence was to be maintained until sight contact with the enemy was made. That was the extent of my instructions.

—Lieutenant Commander Wade McClusky, USS *Enterprise*

A MERE SIX MONTHS AFTER THE DEVASTATION at Pearl Harbor, Japanese Admiral Chuichi Nagumo once again had an opportunity to destroy a massive chunk of the United States Navy all at once with a surprise attack.

It was around ten AM on June 4, 1942. Admiral Nagumo was the guy in charge of the Japanese Aircraft Carrier Fleet off the coast of Midway Island, a tiny hunk of sand in the middle of the Pacific. Midway is home to a US airfield and randomly happens to be one of the world's biggest habitats for albatrosses, green sea turtles, and monk seals (which, of course, are the second-cutest kind of seal, behind harp seals). In a repeat of the insanely successful sucker punch sneak attack at Pearl Harbor, Nagumo and the Japanese fleet had left from Japan, maintained radio silence all the way across the Pacific, and brought hundreds of aircraft to craterize the island's defenses with gigantic high-explosive bombs. Launching from four of Japan's prized aircraft carriers, 108 fighters and bombers filled the skies over Midway with explosions and misery, blasting American hangars, runways, and radar positions into smoking rubble. A couple of Marines on the island managed to get airborne in their Wildcat fighters, but they were colossally outnumbered and were quickly pumped full of lead by the Japanese Zero pilots barreling toward them from all directions. The rest of the Marines' planes were smashed to bits by strafing runs as they sat on the tarmac.

Waiting patiently in the distance, over a hundred Japanese assault craft were packed with infantry troops ready to storm the island, capture it, and set up a Japanese refueling base. It was important to control Midway because the island was within striking distance of Hawaii—and possibly even the West Coast of the United States.

Admiral Nagumo and his boss, Admiral Isoroku Yamamoto, knew that a Japanese base one thousand miles from Hawaii

wasn't the sort of thing the Americans were going to be too happy about. So when a swarm of US torpedo bombers came streaking in on a virtual suicide run to take out the Japanese carriers, neither admiral was all that surprised.

Although none could doubt their incredible bravery, the American wave of Devastator torpedo bombers barreling into the Japanese fleet never stood a chance. Slow, outdated, and hard to maneuver thanks to the two-thousand-pound bomb on their undercarriage, the Devastators were easy prey for the veteran Zero pilots who pounced on them. Diving in from the sun at 330 miles an hour, the Japanese combat air patrol blasted the American squadrons apart, annihilating three separate waves of US torpedo planes without suffering a single loss. Of the forty-one Devastators that took off from the US carriers *Yorktown*, *Hornet*, and *Enterprise*, only six aircraft returned. Only one torpedo hit its target, and that one failed to explode. It just dinged off the ship's hull and sank harmlessly to the bottom of the Pacific.

Admirals Nagumo and Yamamoto were pretty pleased by this, and they were even more excited now that they knew the American navy must be nearby. When a reconnaissance aircraft (also known as a recon aircraft, used for scouting and observation) reported back to Nagumo that they'd found the last three surviving aircraft carriers in the US Pacific Fleet, Nagumo changed course to intercept and crush them once and for all. Val and Kate bombers were lined up on the flight decks of the Japanese carriers *Akagi*, *Kaga*, *Hiryu*, and *Soryu*. Flight crews worked furiously to rearm them with armor-piercing, ship-killing torpedoes for their glorious counterattack. Nagumo told his crews he wanted his bombers in the air immediately. It seemed as though the Japanese navy was about to destroy all that remained of the American fleet and make it back to their ships in time for lunch.

Right around this time, the first Japanese flight crewman looked up to see the front propeller of a United States Navy SBD-3 Dauntless dive-bomber break through the cloud cover and barrel down toward him at 250 miles an hour.

US Douglas SBD-3 Dauntless dive-bombers at Midway, 1942

Lieutenant Commander Clarence Wade McClusky Jr. was a forty-year-old US Navy fighter pilot from Buffalo, New York, and he had been assigned command of Air Group Six aboard the USS *Enterprise*. At the head of two squadrons of SBD Dauntless attack aircraft, McClusky had taken off from the flight deck a couple of hours earlier with orders to attack the Japanese fleet. Unfortunately, when he arrived at the place where they were supposed to be, the Japanese weren't there. McClusky wasn't in the mood to ask for directions like some kind of tourist, so he ordered his men to look for any sign of the enemy. Acting on a hunch, he veered his squadrons away from Midway Island and started scanning the horizon with his binoculars.

After hours of flying and with his fuel reserves alarmingly low, McClusky suddenly noticed a single tiny speck dotting the endless blue sea. Flying closer, he saw that the Japanese destroyer *Arashi* was racing ahead at full flank speed, oblivious to the deadly formation flying high above it. The *Arashi* had broken away from the Japanese fleet a few hours back to fight off an American submarine, but McClusky didn't know this and decided to follow it.

The *Arashi* led him right to the heart of the Japanese carrier fleet at the exact moment when all its fighter planes were down at sea level finishing off the last of the doomed US torpedo bombers. The Japanese Mitsubishi A6M Zeros were some of the fastest and most effective fighter planes in the world, but even at top speed it would have taken them seven minutes to climb from sea level to fifteen thousand feet to engage McClusky's bombers.

He wasn't going to give them the chance.

The bombers' 1,200-horsepower engines violently roared to life as McClusky rolled his plane onto its side and accelerated into a 252-mile-per-hour dive with his nose pointed almost straight down. Behind him, thirty-two aircraft followed suit, each one aiming for a red rising sun painted on the deck of a Japanese carrier.

Dive-bombing in World War II was like a cross between the

Blue Angels and a suicide attempt. Basically, your aircraft starts at fifteen thousand feet, roughly half the altitude of a commercial airliner. Then you do half a barrel roll, turning your plane upside down so you're looking up at the ocean, and you dive at a seventy-degree angle at full speed through a field of antiaircraft flak and heavy machine-gun fire. If the bullets don't kill you, your plane doesn't break apart from the crazy amount of stress you're putting on it, and you don't physically black out, barf, or panic, you then somehow get to just a thousand feet above the ground, hit the button that releases 2,250 pounds of bombs, and hammer back on the flight stick as hard as you possibly can. If you manage to withstand a force nine times the strength of gravity crushing your entire body like a roller coaster from hell, all you have to do is hope your plane pulls up before you crash into the ground and explode into a gigantic fireball. It's basically bungee jumping with a bomb strapped to you, and the planes scream just like in old movies when they're on fire and going down.

Now imagine dozens of aircraft doing this in unison, one wave after another, through a sky filled with tracer gunfire, black smoke, and airburst flak explosions. They dive straight toward the three Japanese aircraft carriers whose flight decks are loaded up with gasoline trucks, bombs, and antiship torpedoes.

Fireworks.

Wade McClusky's vision came back into focus as he leveled out his dive, dropped his Dauntless to a mere twenty feet above the water, and thrust his throttle forward so hard he was basically pushing it through the plane's control console. Behind him, he heard explosion after explosion as Japanese aircraft carriers, caught completely unprepared, were wracked by dozens of direct hits from devastating explosive bombs. The *Kaga* and *Soryu* were burning all across their decks. The *Akagi*, crippled by a direct hit that penetrated all the way through the deck, was already tilted to its side and sinking into the sea.

But McClusky wasn't out of the fire just yet. As he was admiring his handiwork, tracer fire zipped past his cockpit, splashing up the water below him. The naval aviator looked up to see two Zeros closing in on him, and the Japanese pilots were pretty righteously angry about getting their homes blown to smithereens.

Diving and weaving at such low altitudes that his wing tips practically touched the water, McClusky evaded the two Zeros. In the backseat of the cockpit, his radio operator opened fire with a rear-facing .30-caliber machine gun, spewing hundreds of rounds of ammunition at the attackers. After nearly five minutes of a white-knuckle firefight, McClusky's gunner found his mark, blasting a Zero so hard that the impact broke the cockpit on McClusky's Dauntless. When he landed on the *Enterprise* later that day, McClusky counted fifty-five bullet and shrapnel holes in his aircraft.

By the time the battle ended, four Japanese aircraft carriers were at the bottom of the sea. With them went 250 airplanes and 3,000 sailors, many of whom were critical mechanics and flight crew servicing Japanese aircraft. The United States lost one carrier, the USS *Yorktown*, which was hit by bombers and submarines later in the day, but the victory was decisive and complete. It was a demoralizing loss for the Japanese, the first defeat they'd suffered at the hands of a foreign power in 250 years. The Midway invasion fleet was called off, and the Japanese suddenly found themselves on the defensive.

The USS *Yorktown* on fire during the Battle of Midway, 1942

WADE McCLUSKY

For his actions at Midway, Lieutenant Commander Wade McClusky received the Navy Cross, the second-highest award for bravery given by the US Navy. He commanded an escort carrier later in the war, served as chief of staff to a couple of fleet commanders during the Korean War, and retired in 1956 at the rank of rear admiral. Nowadays the Wade McClusky Award is given out every year to the best attack squadron in the US Navy.

Captain Clarence Wade McClusky Jr., c. 1943

THE FIGHT FOR ALASKA

To distract the United States from Midway, the Japanese simultaneously launched an attack on the Aleutian Islands in Alaska. Setting up bases on the deserted islands of Attu and Kiska, they were able to launch raids on the US naval bases at Unalaska and Dutch Harbor. The Japanese held the islands for nearly a year, but in May 1943 they counterattacked an American landing with a thousand-man suicide charge through snow and mud in the mountains that ultimately proved unsuccessful.

SABURO SAKAI

The most famous fighter pilot in the Japanese navy was Saburo Sakai, a high-octane Zero pilot who got his start strafing US aircraft with bullets in the skies over the Philippines in 1941. An expert marksman and a daring flier, Sakai had already shot down sixty enemy aircraft when he was shot in the head and immediately paralyzed in half his body. But Sakai managed to land his burning aircraft safely and escape, and he was back in the cockpit of a Zero less than a year later. Living by the code "Never give up," Sakai was wounded four times in battle but fought through the end of the war, spending the last years taking on American bombers that were attacking mainland Japan. Of the 150 pilots in his unit at the beginning of the war, only 3 survived until the end.

READING THEIR TEXTS

Perhaps the single greatest advantage the Allies had over the Axis was that they were able to crack the secret codes the Japanese and Germans were using to communicate military activities. Pretty much anyone who had the right equipment was able to pick up enemy radio signals or read their e-mails (well, telegraphs, but basically the same thing), so militaries had to use complicated codes so that even if the bad guys were listening, they still wouldn't know what the heck you were talking about. But British and Polish cryptologists working in the UK's Government Code and Cypher School managed to unscramble the Nazi Enigma code, while the US Army Signals Intelligence Service built themselves a similar secret decoder ring–style device to translate Japanese commands. This basically allowed the Allies to read the enemy game plan anytime those guys were silly enough to send it via radio or telegraph. And thanks to clever use of the information that didn't make it obvious the Allies had it, the Japanese *never figured out* that their enemy could hear and understand everything they were saying!

As an awesome side note, the Americans disguised Allied signals by employing members of the Navajo tribe to design a code using their native language. Since nobody outside the Navajo Nation could speak fluent Navajo, the Japanese were never able to decipher what exactly was going on with the Americans.

THE FLYING TIGERS

Streaking through the skies above war-torn China, the pilots of the American Volunteer Group, better known as the "Flying Tigers," spent the early parts of 1942 making life in China miserable for the occupying armies of Imperial Japan.

The AVG was initially set up in the summer of 1941, a solid six months before the Japanese attacked Pearl Harbor. It was commanded by Claire Lee Chennault, an iron-jawed Texan who had retired from the United States Army Air Force in 1937 at the fairly low rank of captain. Chennault was in China working as a military adviser to Chinese Nationalist leader Chiang Kai-Shek after the Japanese attacked Shanghai, and he decided he was going to do something to help. Since the United States wasn't at war with Japan, he couldn't request US troops, so he put out a call for veteran pilots looking for adventure and excitement to sign up with his unofficial outfit and shoot down Japanese fighter planes. He also offered five hundred bucks for every Japanese plane they took out.

Chennault recruited about three hundred pilots, mechanics, and ground crew and divided them up into three squadrons—two in China and one in Burma (present-day Myanmar). Equipped with top-of-the-line supercharged

P-40B Warhawk fighter planes (which the Chinese government bought from the United States) that had awesome-looking shark mouths painted on their sides, the American Volunteer Group immediately hurled themselves into the action with their .50-caliber machine guns blazing. They went on missions to attack enemy ground forces, blew up Japanese bases, laid down murderous curtains of fire to cover Chinese Army attacks, and caused chaos among enemy bomber fleets. Before long, the combination of heroic bravery and cool-as-heck toothy paint jobs led the Chinese and the international media to know the American Volunteer Group simply as the "Flying Tigers."

For six months the Tigers operated out of small, underequipped bases hidden deep in the jungles and countryside of China, striking quickly, raking the enemy with quad-machine-gun fire, and then peeling out at nearly four hundred miles per hour before enemy reinforcements could show up. In one battle on Christmas Day 1942, American pilot "Duke" Hedman and his wingman found themselves locked up in combat with an entire squadron of Japanese army attack planes. Cranking out thousands of bullets while hurtling through the rain at 340 miles an hour, Hedman blasted apart enemy aircraft that were so close to him he had to do barrel rolls just to avoid crashing into their burning wreckage. Hedman was a guy better known for playing the piano and singing bad show tunes at the Tigers' favorite bar, but somehow he dodged and dove and took out four enemy fighters in just a few minutes. Suddenly, a Japanese machine-gun bullet broke through the cockpit and embedded itself in the headrest just inches from Hedman's face. But this steel-nerved daredevil didn't panic—he turned, dove, and shot down the guy who'd hit him. For shooting down five enemy planes in a single encounter, Hedman became the United States' first "ace in a day."

In the six months between when the Tigers got started in December 1941 and their breakup in July 1942, they claimed to have shot down 299 Japanese aircraft, nailed 240 on the ground, and blown up dozens of enemy bases and transport ships, all with just 19 pilots killed or captured. Chennault's Tigers would eventually take on more men, become part of the United States Fourteenth Air Force, and serve out the rest of the war as the Twenty-Third Fighter Group. The grateful Chinese soldiers never stopped referring to the men as Flying Tigers.

KNOW YOUR VEHICLES

	USS *Enterprise*	IJN *Akagi*
TYPE	*Yorktown*-class aircraft carrier	Aircraft carrier
COUNTRY	United States	Japan
COMMISSIONED	1938	1927
LENGTH	809 feet, 5 inches	855 feet, 3 inches
DISPLACEMENT	17,900 tons	32,850 tons
ARMOR	122 millimeters	152 millimeters
ENGINE	4 Parsons geared steam turbines	4 Kampon geared steam turbines
TOP SPEED	37 mph	36 mph
CREW	2,919	1,630
AIRCRAFT	18 F4F Wildcats, 18 TBDs, and 36 Dauntless	18 Zeros, 18 D3A Vals, and 36 B5N Kates
ARMAMENT	Eight 5-inch cannons Sixteen 40mm antiaircraft guns Forty-four 20mm antiaircraft guns	Six 8-inch cannons Twelve 120mm antiaircraft guns Twenty-eight 25mm antiaircraft guns

The Japanese aircraft carrier *Akagi* was bigger and heavier than the American carrier *Enterprise,* and it had a really cool design with three flight decks stacked on top of one another. This meant that planes could take off on one deck, be repaired on another, and land on the third all at the same time. The carriers each had four squadrons of aircraft—one squadron of eighteen fighters, and three squadrons of attack craft like dive-bombers or torpedo planes. The *Enterprise*, the "Big E," was a veteran of twenty battles in the Pacific, surviving so many harrowing situations that Japanese military intelligence mistakenly reported it as being sunk on three separate occasions.

★★★ 8 ★★★

STALINGRAD

The Bloodiest Battle in Human History

Stalingrad, Russia

August 19, 1942–February 2, 1943

There is no ground for us beyond the Volga.

—Lieutenant Vasily Zaitsev, Soviet Sixty-Second Army

FURIOUS OVER THE SETBACKS SUFFERED BY HIS forces across the Eastern Front, in the middle of 1942 Hitler rage-fired a bunch of his top commanders. He then assumed overall control of the German military, which is interesting because he never advanced beyond the rank of corporal while he was actually *in* the German Army. Nobody was dumb enough to argue with the Führer, though, and in the fall of 1942 Hitler ordered his troops to launch a massive, all-out attack on the heavily populated Russian city of Stalingrad.

The attack was designed to completely dismantle the city—brick by brick if necessary.

Sure, it was going to be awesome to completely obliterate a city named after Stalin, Hitler's archnemesis. But Stalingrad was important for way more than just totalitarian dictator bragging rights. For starters, the sprawling city was home to dozens of factories and produced a quarter of all the trucks, tractors, and tanks in the Soviet army. On top of that, it was situated along the Volga River in the Caucasus region of southern Russia. Capturing the city would allow Hitler's troops to blitzkrieg into the rich oil fields of the Caucasus Mountains and grab a ton of resources to make gas for their tanks and airplanes.

On August 19, 1942, soldiers from General Friedrich Paulus's German Sixth Army crossed the Don River and began their march on the city of Stalingrad. The only Russians stationed in the suburbs outside the city were the soldiers of the 1077th Antiaircraft Regiment—an all-female unit of peasant women and girls. Their primary job was to take potshots at German bombers as they sailed overhead. The 1077th wasn't trained or equipped to deal with a ground attack, yet these brave women still defiantly opened fire on the tanks of the German Sixteenth Panzer Division. They were no match for the Germans but heroically fought to the end, the last women dying at their guns. Each one hoped her sacrifice would buy time for the Russians to move up reinforcements and organize the city's defenses.

Before the war, Vasily Zaitsev of the 1047th Rifle Regiment, Soviet Sixty-Second Army, had been a hunter (his family was so poor that they couldn't afford to waste ammo and taught him to kill with one shot) and a shepherd living in the foothills of the Ural Mountains. When hunting deer in subzero Siberian weather wasn't exciting enough for him, Zaitsev enlisted in the military but was given some boring desk job doing paperwork for the Russian Navy in the middle of nowhere. Once things started getting intense with the war, Zaitsev requested a transfer to frontline work so he could actually start shooting Nazis.

He was thrown headfirst into what would become the single deadliest military action in human history.

Like many reinforcement soldiers hurled into the meat grinder at Stalingrad, Zaitsev got his introduction to the city when he was taken across the Volga River in an unarmed, repurposed old ferryboat that was being used for target practice by Nazi artillery. With the still-burning rubble of Stalingrad clearly visible on the far bank, Zaitsev and hundreds of other Russian troops (none of whom even had guns yet) drifted across the mighty river in a boat that up until recently had been used to take tourists sightseeing. Artillery shells splashed up huge columns of water as dozens of other ships frantically brought men to the battlefield, while up above, the terrifying scream of Stuka dive-bombers signaled impending death. German planes strafed the boats with machine guns, dropped bombs onto ferries, and blew ships and men sky-high to keep them from crossing the river.

Vasily Zaitsev was one of the lucky guys who made it to the other side of the Volga River, but this only made his situation worse. The Soviet Union was in a weird position where they had more people than guns, so at Stalingrad the deal was that one soldier received a rifle and the guy next to him received a handful of bullets. When they handed Zaitsev his clip, they told him to just grab a gun off a dead body once he got out there. "Okay, guys, sounds like fun." He was then immediately thrown into battle and ordered to charge in a gnarly human wave attack straight into fortified German machine-gun positions. If he lost his nerve and retreated, his own men would shoot him as a coward and a traitor.

The resulting assault was heroic and senseless. The Russian infantry, half of whom didn't even have guns, were brutally cut down while charging across open ground toward the German front lines. Zaitsev somehow managed to survive.

Welcome to Stalingrad, Comrade.

The grand, sweeping tank attacks of the German blitzkrieg didn't really work when the battle was being fought between guys shooting at one another across the street. So Stalingrad soon became known to the Germans as *Rattenkrieg*—"Rat War." With the entire city burning, covered in smoke and rubble, and being shelled and bombed by both armies, soldiers fought house to house and room to room with everything from grenades and guns to knives and shovels. It wasn't uncommon for opposing forces to occupy different floors in the same apartment building or for troops to get mixed up and accidentally end up holding positions that were already behind enemy lines. Tanks couldn't pass through the blasted-out buildings, but the ruins provided tons of cover to infantry. They were also loaded with booby traps and led to groups of men stumbling into one another and fighting at ridiculously close range. The average Soviet army private was expected to survive for just *twenty-four hours* on the battlefield.

German soldiers defending a structure in Stalingrad

It was dark, bloody, and ugly. It was also the perfect environment for a new kind of warrior to make his way onto the scene: the sniper—an elite marksman, perfectly hidden among the debris of the ruined city, who could kill with a single shot and then melt into the shadows and disappear.

An expert hunter and master marksman, Junior Lieutenant Vasily Zaitsev became one of the best and most successful snipers in the history of warfare after surviving the charge straight into German machine-gun fire. Moving through the sewers or along rooftops and going days without food or rest, Zaitsev made his way to firing positions throughout the city in an effort to find a worthwhile target. Lying motionless for hours in freezing cold rubble, Zaitsev waited for the perfect shot, preferring to take out German officers, machine gunners, and other high-profile enemies. Hiding in abandoned pipes, bombed-out towers, and ruined factories, Zaitsev picked off Nazis one after another, vaporizing soldiers' morale and killing their leaders almost at will. In his first ten days in Stalingrad, Zaitsev had already picked off forty Germans and, thanks to the Russian propaganda machine putting out newspapers about his exploits, he was also becoming a legend among the people of the Soviet Union.

Zaitsev was so good at killing from long-range distances with a scoped sniper rifle, he eventually set up a mini–sniper school in the heart of Stalingrad to give shooters some on-the-job training. Taking on somewhere between twenty and thirty soldiers (both men and women!), Zaitsev trained his sniper cadre in a burned-out factory, then had them work together in teams of two or three, hunting Germans across the city. Before long, his snipers were terrorizing the Germans left and right, stalling their attacks and making them think twice every time they popped their heads up from a trench.

In just four months, Vasily Zaitsev recorded 242 confirmed kills, including 11 enemy snipers—some of whom had specifically been sent to track him down and kill him. There's a story out there about a German war hero named Major Koenig who was dispatched straight from Berlin to face Zaitsev one-on-one

Vasily Zaitsev (in foreground) training snipers in Stalingrad, 1942

in an awesome Stalingrad sniper duel, but most historians are pretty sure this was made up to promote the legend of Zaitsev among the Russian population. In the story, Zaitsev hunts Koenig for three days through the ruined buildings of Stalingrad, then tricks him by putting a hat on a stick, holding it up, and getting Koenig to shoot the hat. When Koenig shoots, Zaitsev can see the flash from his gun and takes him down. Like I said, it's probably not true, but it's still a cool story.

The Russian army fought for their lives in the ruins of Stalingrad over the course of eight long, brutal months. Tanks were rolling out of factories straight into battle before they even had time to be painted. Troops were being thrown to the front from all across Russia to stem the German tide. To give you some idea of the scale of this epic, war-changing engagement, during the battle, an estimated two million people were killed, wounded, or taken prisoner. According to the 2010 US Census, that's more than the total population of fifteen US states!

Finally, in November 1942, the tide turned decisively against the Nazis. A million fresh Soviet troops rolled in from the north, surrounding General Friedrich Paulus's Sixth Army in Stalingrad. Paulus requested permission to break out of the trap, but Hitler demanded he hold his ground, so Paulus fought on for three more months. But it was useless. In February 1943 he surrendered all that remained of the German Sixth Army.

Russian troops fighting for Stalingrad

He was the highest-ranking German officer to surrender his command, and the fall of his army would mark the turning point of World War II.

PAVLOV'S HOUSE

Another famous defender of Stalingrad was Sergeant Jacob Pavlov of the Forty-Second Rifle Regiment. Ordered to hold an apartment building in downtown Stalingrad just barely on the German side of the Volga River, Pavlov and his twenty-five-man platoon battled nonstop enemy attacks for fifty-nine long days. Pavlov blew out the floors of the building so his men could pass ammo up and down through the structure, set up sniper positions on the roof and machine-gun nests in every window, and even brought up a wheeled antitank cannon to fire out of his basement. The building was code-named Lighthouse because tracer fire lit up the skies around it every night; the joke among the Russians was that the Germans lost more men attacking "Pavlov's House" than they lost attacking Paris.

DEADLY UMBRELLA

Horrified and impressed by the success of Russian snipers at Stalingrad, German commanders started implementing a sniper program of their own. One of the most successful soldiers in the program was Josef Allerberger, an Austrian machine gunner who was brought in to cover the retreat of German forces from southern Russia in 1943. Hiding behind an umbrella painted with camouflage and decorated with foliage, Allerberger stalled enemy attacks, took out Red Army officers, and went on special missions to battle Soviet snipers. He was credited with 257 kills during the war.

NO PITY

The ninety-one thousand survivors of the German Sixth Army became prisoners of the Soviet Union. The Russians, who were furious over German atrocities in the war, transferred these prisoners to Siberia and interned (confined) them in Stalin's brutal forced-labor camps. Harsh conditions in subzero temperatures would take a horrifying toll on the already exhausted men. Only five thousand of these soldiers would ever return home to Germany.

THE SIEGE OF LENINGRAD

German troops encircled the city of Leningrad (modern-day St. Petersburg) on September 8, 1941. Settling in for an old-school, Viking-style siege, the Germans blocked all roads into the city, cut off the food and coal supply, and started launching bombs and artillery shells day and night. They figured it was only a matter of time until the residents couldn't take any more and surrendered. Except that this never happened. The Nazis waited two and a half years—nearly nine hundred days!—outside the city, while the citizens of Leningrad starved, froze, caught horrible diseases, or were killed by bombs. As thousands of their fellow Russians' bodies lined the streets around them, courageous survivors melted snow for water, burned libraries for heat, and ate rats, zoo animals, and even their own dead to survive. Despite horrific conditions that killed fifty-three thousand people in December 1941 alone, the city and its defenders stubbornly resisted the German invaders. Many of the old and sick were evacuated in January 1942 when Lake Ladoga froze solid, but others remained. By the time the Red Army drove the Germans off in January 1944, over a million Russians had died within the city walls.

KNOW YOUR VEHICLES

	Ilyushin IL-2 Sturmovik	Polikarpov Po-2
TYPE	Ground attack aircraft	Ground attack aircraft
COUNTRY	Soviet Union	Soviet Union
FIRST PRODUCED	1941	1929
LENGTH	38 feet, 1 inch	26 feet, 10 inches
WEIGHT	14,065 pounds	2,271 pounds
ARMOR	12 millimeters	None
ENGINE	1,720-hp Mikulin AM-38F V-12	125-hp Shvetsov M-11D 5-cylinder radial
TOP SPEED	257 mph	94 mph
RATE OF CLIMB	2,050 feet per minute	546 feet per minute
CREW	2	2
ARMAMENT	Two 23mm cannons; two forward 7.62mm machine guns; one rear-facing 12.7mm machine gun; eight 82mm RS-82 rockets; up to 1,320 pounds of bombs	One 7.62mm machine gun Six 110-pound bombs

To smash German ground forces, the Soviets used two main attack bombers: the heavily armored, rocket-equipped, ultratough IL-2 Sturmovik ground attack fighter, and a dinky little wood-and-canvas biplane called the Po-2. During the day IL-2s would dive in, cannons blazing, as enemy guns bounced off their armor plating. Then, at night, the Po-2s—many of which were piloted by women known as the "Night Witches"—would glide in under cover of darkness with their engines off and drop bombs on the Germans while they slept. The Po-2 was so slow that German planes literally could not slow down to its speed without stalling and crashing. Of course, it was also so cheaply made that a soldier on the ground could shoot through the canvas wings with an infantry rifle.

9

SEMPER FI

The Battle for Henderson Field

Guadalcanal, Solomon Islands
October 23–26, 1942

I continued the trigger bursts until the barrel began to steam. In front of me was a large pile of dead bodies. I ran around the ridge from gun to gun trying to keep each gun firing, but at each emplacement I only found dead Marine gunners. I knew then that I must be all alone.

—Sergeant Mitchell Paige, Second Battalion, Seventh Marines

THE RAIN WAS POURING DOWN IN SHEETS through the dense jungle foliage. Huge palm trees and canopy jungle obscured any hint of moonlight, leaving the entire landscape a pitch-black slippery mud pit. The sound of the rain splattering on the palm fronds and puddles seemed almost deafening, yet still dozens of ears strained for any hint of what might lie in the inky blackness beyond.

Lying facedown in a half inch of brown water, barely peering over the edge of a protective bulletproof layer of waterlogged sandbags, terrified young men held their breath and waited for the attack they knew was coming.

Then, out of nowhere, a quick flash of light high above the jungle. It was followed immediately by the whistling of artillery shells, the deafening boom of mortar explosions, and the screams of wounded men echoing from seemingly every direction at once.

Deep in the jungle, hundreds of silhouettes appeared. With the violent war cry of "*Banzai!*" (meaning "Ten thousand years," or basically "Long live the emperor"), a human wave of terrifying veteran Japanese warriors surged ahead, their rifle-mounted bayonets, knives, and (in the case of the officers) samurai swords glinting in the light of the gunfire. With bullets and artillery zipping through the night sky, these raging fighters sprinted full speed toward their objective, utterly oblivious to the dangers and death flying around them, not even caring if they lived or died as long as it was glorious.

Muzzle flashes and frantic shouts answered the attack all along the American defensive lines. The shaken, preposterously outnumbered men of the Seventh Marine Regiment, First Marine Division, took aim and opened fire into the sea of death that was quickly threatening to sweep over their positions.

After the overwhelming American victory at Midway, the United States decided to take the fight to the Empire of Japan. The first major American offensive in the Pacific was an assault on the island of Guadalcanal, a twenty-five-hundred-square-mile-wide, jungle-covered death rock off the coast of Papua New Guinea. Situated surprisingly close to places like Fiji and Tahiti that we now think of as tropical resorts with clear blue swimming pools and brightly colored drinks, Guadalcanal was more of a rain-soaked jungle hellhole full of malaria-infected mosquitoes and rampant dysentery. This place was so scenic it was once described by a Marine as "the only place in the world where you can be standing in mud to your knees and still get dust in your eyes." But, hey, the Japanese were building an airfield there so they could launch bombing raids on Australia and New Zealand, and it made sense to go in and start busting heads.

The US plan was pretty awesome: Land on Guadalcanal before the Japanese could finish building their airfield, attack it, steal the airfield, finish building it, and make it an American air base instead. And that's exactly what they did.

On August 7, 1942, a force of eleven thousand US Marines raced toward the shores of Guadalcanal in fast-attack landing craft. Bombs whistled over their heads as US Navy warships hurled gigantic explosive shells into the jungle, but nobody really knew how many Japanese were there or where they were. So the Marines were a little surprised when they didn't

A US Marine guarding a ridge on Guadalcanal, 1942

run into any trouble on the beach. They quickly hustled to the airfield, captured it from a small force of Japanese, renamed it Henderson Field (after the commander of the Marine pilots on Midway Island), and then immediately went to work using bulldozers and equipment to finish constructing the airstrip. Still, there was nothing from the enemy.

That night, things changed.

For the next two and a half months, the Japanese did every single thing they possibly could to rip Henderson Field from the hands of the United States Marine Corps. From dawn until dusk, Japanese ships hurled colossal shells, mortars rained down death, and dive-bombers strafed construction crews and Marine positions without mercy. At night, bomber raids struck at American warships, and fleets of Japanese transports known as the "Tokyo Express" snuck toward the coast and dropped hundreds of fresh soldiers and supplies on the shores of Guadalcanal to join the fight. The Marines dug into defensive positions around Henderson Field and were even able to put together a group of fighter planes known as the "Cactus Air Force" to try to fend off the constant Japanese bombing raids. But the dust and mud made it really tough to take off, land, and keep your plane's gears from getting clogged up. Oh yeah, and also the Japanese were firing artillery pieces that were blowing huge craters into the place where the US pilots were supposed to land, which probably wasn't all that fun, either. The US fleet tried to cut off Japanese sea and air access to the island, but night attacks from dive-bombers severely damaged a half dozen American warships, and they were ordered to back off for their own safety, basically leaving the Marines stranded on an island full of angry people trying to kill them.

The decisive struggles for Henderson Field took place after dark on the nights of October 24, 25, and 26. The Japanese, looking to take advantage of the fact that they ridiculously outnumbered the Americans, waited until pitch-black darkness overtook the land. Then for three nights in a row they sent thousands upon thousands of hardcore, totally fearless soldiers screaming out from the jungles straight into the

Marine Corps' defensive positions. Holding their bayonet-equipped rifles high, flinging grenades around like a beauty queen tossing candy off a float at a New Year's parade, and roaring at the top of their lungs like old-school Viking berserkers, the Japanese in their onslaught were a terrifying sight to behold. If the prospect of being stabbed in the face with a twelve-inch bayonet wielded by a guy descended from a samurai wasn't scary enough, the entire frantic thing was also accompanied by a serious artillery and mortar barrage that sent thousands of high-explosive shells whistling down through the air on top of the Marines out of nowhere.

Across the narrow field separating the jungle from the frighteningly thin American defensive line, Gunnery Sergeant John Basilone cranked the handle of his Browning .30-06-caliber machine gun, gritted his teeth, and let rip a deadly stream of brutal machine-gun fire that scythed into the enemy lines like a lawn mower. An Italian-American kid from New Jersey, "Manila John" had been the US Army boxing champion in the Philippines, but quickly transferred over to the Marines specifically to kick some butt. The fifteen men in his heavy machine-gun section were staring down a force of nearly three thousand Japanese, but this didn't slow down Basilone. Running up and down the lines, he urged his Marines on, continually repositioned his heavy machine guns to get the best firing positions, cleared gun jams, and manned the guns himself when necessary. At one point, a group of Japanese jumped into his foxhole with their bayonets ready, but Gunnery Sergeant Basilone quick-drew his Colt .45 pistol like an Old West gunslinger and put those guys down before they could fire off a round.

All the way on the other side of the airfield, Platoon Sergeant Mitchell Paige of the Second Battalion, Seventh Marines, found himself in a similar situation. The son of Serbian immigrants, an Eagle Scout, a member of the Marine Corps baseball team, and a dude who once punched an off-duty Japanese officer unconscious during a barroom brawl in Beijing, Paige was in command of a thirty-three-man machine-gun platoon that was being almost completely overrun by more than twenty-five hundred Japanese infantrymen. Spewing sweeping arcs of fire straight into the teeth of the enemy charge, Paige's weapon was practically glowing red from the heat of the barrel, yet still he fought on. With most of his crew dead at their positions, Paige ran back and forth through the dark trenches, firing each gun to try to confuse the enemy about how many men he still had alive. When the two companies to his right were pushed back by the attack and retreated, Paige found himself face-to-face with a Japanese infantryman who rushed forward and jammed the bayonet at his neck. Paige put his hand up to deflect the strike, almost losing two fingers in the process, but managed to draw his standard-issue Marine combat knife and kill the dude with it.

The second he turned away, he saw a Japanese soldier

standing ten feet from him with a machine gun at the ready. Paige dove to his back as the enemy soldier ripped off a burst of gunfire, the bullets slicing so close to Paige's face that he could feel the heat from them, but somehow he avoided the shot and returned fire, killing the enemy gunner. But there was no time to think. He jumped back to his feet and ran to the next gun position to continue fighting.

Back at the First Battalion, several hours of nonstop fighting had started to take their toll on John Basilone's section as well. The gunnery sergeant ran down his lines to find that all but three of his men had been killed, and a hand of one of those three survivors had been blown off by an enemy grenade. Worse, Basilone's guys were almost completely out of bullets for their machine guns, and there were reports that Japanese infantry had broken through and were running around *behind* Basilone's position.

Manila John didn't care. He needed ammo to keep up the fight, and he was going to get it. He sprinted back through the darkness toward the supply tent, charging through the dense jungle at top speed. During his mad dash, Basilone crashed into someone, knocking both the other man and himself to the mud.

The dude was a Japanese officer, and he was with a couple of his guys.

John Basilone killed them with his pistol and his bare hands. He then got to the supply base, grabbed as much ammo as he could carry, and ran back through the confusion to the front lines to resupply his men and continue working the guns.

Not long after that, Mitchell Paige found himself in some brutal hand-to-hand combat as well. After ten hours of nonstop white-knuckle battle at extremely close ranges, dawn was finally approaching, and the platoon sergeant could see that every single man in his unit had been killed in the fighting. With the Japanese regrouping on the other side of a ridge, Paige decided he was done waiting for them to come to him. He lifted his red-hot, 103-pound machine gun off its tripod, threw two belts of ammunition around his neck, and yelled for a nearby Marine rifle team to "fix bayonets and follow me!"

Paige hustled over the ridge, lugging the gun like something out of an awesome eighties action movie. He was followed quickly by a half dozen guys with bayonets at the ready. On the other side he found a field of tall grass, and the second Paige opened fire he saw eighteen Japanese guys pop up in ambush and run toward him yelling at the top of their lungs with their bayonets out.

Paige cut them all down, firing thirteen hundred rounds per minute of large-caliber ammunition while holding the gun low around his waist. When the enemy squad's commander pitched forward into the mud, he was about five steps away from chopping Paige down with a samurai sword.

The Marines around Henderson Field miraculously held the line despite being brutally outnumbered and suffering severe casualties. During seventy-two hours of constant fighting, with no sleep, rest, or food, these men held off a force many times their size and stayed firm even as their friends were being cut down left and right. Henderson Field stayed in American hands throughout the war. And the Japanese had now suffered their first defeat in a land battle since the days of the samurai over a hundred years earlier.

Both John Basilone and Mitchell Paige went on to receive the United States' highest award for military bravery—the Medal of Honor—for their actions on Guadalcanal in October 1942. Both men are now considered legendary in Marine Corps history.

Second Lieutenant Mitchell Paige

Sergeant John Basilone

PT-109

To combat the Tokyo Express, the US Navy started using maneuverable little torpedo boats known as PTs (Patrol Torpedo boats) that could patrol narrow inlets and coastal areas. Their mission was to search for and destroy Japanese transports and supply boats. One such ship, PT-109, was waiting to ambush Japanese craft off the coast of the Solomon Islands in 1943 when it was suddenly rammed by a Japanese destroyer that came out of nowhere and split the PT boat in half. Two of the seventeen crewmen on the tiny boat were killed in the crash. But the ship's captain, Lieutenant Junior Grade (and future US president) John F. Kennedy, and his crew swam four hours to the shore of a nearby island, with Kennedy dragging a wounded comrade behind him all the way. The crew scrounged for food and evaded capture on the island for seven days before finally being rescued.

SPORTS IN 1942

In 1942 the best hitter in baseball was Ted Williams of the Boston Red Sox. Williams had a batting average over .400 in 1941, a tremendous feat that hasn't been duplicated since. Immediately following that season, however, Williams quit baseball, enlisted in the Marine Corps, and spent the war serving as a combat aviator. Around this time, the best baseball teams were the St. Louis Cardinals, led by Stan Musial, and the New York Yankees, who rocked Joe DiMaggio in their batting order and had Spud Chandler pitching.

The NFL only had ten teams at this point, no Super Bowl, and players wore leather helmets without face masks and played both offense and defense. The NFL Championships were dominated by the Chicago Bears, led by QB Sid Luckman, and the Washington Redskins, quarterbacked by "Slingin' Sammy" Baugh. He not only threw twenty-three touchdown passes in 1943 but also set an NFL record by intercepting eleven passes as a defensive back. The 1942 NFL MVP was Don Hutson of the Green Bay Packers, a wide receiver who set NFL records with seventy-four catches for 1,211 yards, and seventeen touchdowns.

LOCAL HERO

Many native Solomon Islanders living on Guadalcanal provided valuable intelligence to the American forces. One of these guys, a man named Jacob Vouza, was captured by the Japanese, who ruthlessly tortured him for hours to get him to give up the location of the American forces. When Vouza refused, the Japanese tied him to a post and bayoneted him through the face, neck, stomach, and both of his arms, then left him to die. After they were gone, Vouza chewed through the ropes with his teeth, crawled to the American lines, and got there just in time to warn the Marines that five hundred Japanese soldiers were on their way. The Marines ran to their defenses and easily turned back the enemy attack ten minutes later.

SMOKEY JOE

The most successful pilot of the Cactus Air Force was Joe Foss, commander of Marine F4F Wildcat fighter squadron VMF-121. A super-aggressive pilot who loved chewing cigars in the cockpit while dogfighting Japanese Zeros, Foss had a favorite tactic: to get close enough to "leave powder burns on their fuselage" and then open fire from less than fifty yards away (which is not very far when you're flying at three hundred miles an hour several thousand feet above the ground). Fearlessly taking on bombers and fighters, and strafing Japanese boats, "Smokey Joe" Foss shot down twenty-six enemy planes over Guadalcanal. He also survived being shot down in shark-infested waters off the coast. After the war, he made friends with Hollywood action hero John Wayne, wrote three books on dogfighting, and served as the director of the Air Force Academy, the president of the National Rifle Association, and the commissioner of the football league that became the NFL's AFC.

MATANIKAU RIVER

One of the first big battles on Guadalcanal happened along the Matanikau River, when two companies of the First Battalion, Seventh Marines, were ambushed and cut off by a fearsome force of Japanese troops. The battalion commander, Marine legend "Chesty" Puller (a five-time Navy Cross recipient so tough that when they first showed him a flamethrower, all he said was "Where the hell do you put the bayonet?"), demanded that his men be evacuated. But his superiors said that it was too dangerous and that those units were lost. Puller, a cranky Virginian and a veteran of Marine Corps battles in Haiti, China, and Nicaragua, growled, "You're not going to throw these men away!" He then flagged down a US Navy destroyer and ordered the crew to commence operations to rescue the stranded companies.

Even though Puller had absolutely no authority to do it, the destroyer agreed, and ten landing craft were deployed to evacuate the Marines. When the evacuation came under heavy fire from enemy troops in the jungle, one ultrabrave Coast Guard officer named Douglas Munro heroically put his small gunboat between the landing craft and the Japanese to shield the evacuation from enemy fire. Munro was killed in action, but five hundred Marines were saved from certain death thanks to his actions. To this day, Munro remains the only member of the United States Coast Guard ever to receive the Medal of Honor.

KNOW YOUR VEHICLES

	USS *San Francisco*	IJN *Hiei*
TYPE	*New Orleans*–class heavy cruiser	*Kongo*-class battleship
COUNTRY	United States	Japan
COMMISSIONED	1934	1914
LENGTH	588 feet, 2 inches	728 feet, 4 inches
DISPLACEMENT	9,950 tons	37,187 tons
ARMOR	127 millimeters	203 millimeters
ENGINE	Four Parsons/Westinghouse geared turbines	Two steam turbines
TOP SPEED	32 knots (37 mph)	30 knots (35 mph)
CREW	708	1,360
ARMAMENT	Nine 8-inch cannons Eight 5-inch cannons Eight .50-caliber machine guns	Eight 14-inch cannons Sixteen 6-inch cannons Eight 5-inch cannons Twenty 25mm antiaircraft autocannons

The Japanese attempted to land troops on Guadalcanal and open fire on Henderson Field with battleship cannons, but in the middle of the night they ran straight into a convoy of American cruisers and destroyers led by the USS *San Francisco*. In fighting so close that opposing ships had to swerve to avoid crashing into one another, four American cruisers and eight destroyers slugged it out with two Japanese battleships, a cruiser, and nine destroyers. Both sides were battered mercilessly from every direction in a ruthless engagement that left the American admiral dead and the Japanese admiral wounded. But the Japanese were driven back from the waterway. The Americans lost four destroyers, and basically every other ship was heavily damaged. The Japanese flagship *Hiei* was also sunk, as well as two Japanese destroyers.

10

FIGHTING WITH TIGERS

The Battle of Kursk

July 5–August 23, 1943
Kursk, Russia

History shows that there are no invincible armies and that there never have been.

—Soviet premier Josef Stalin

CHURNING UP THE BARREN RUSSIAN LANDSCAPE at thirty-four miles per hour, Lieutenant Samusenko of the First Guards Tank Army glared through the T-34's gunsights at the rapidly approaching formation of hulking enemy panzers. Samusenko was unfazed as explosions mulched up the countryside, dive-bombers screamed overhead, and armor-piercing shells whizzed past the turret.

The lieutenant was just one among an 840-vehicle-wide sea of Soviet T-34 medium tanks hurled into action against the best-equipped, most fanatical troops Adolf Hitler had to offer. With little less than the survival of Mother Russia on the line, Lieutenant Samusenko calmly ordered the vehicle's driver to accelerate to maximum speed and the loader to slam another 76.2mm antitank shell into the main cannon.

Sometimes in war—and especially in a brutal, bloody, gruesome, no-holds-barred war between two countries that hate each other with an ungodly death-rage—you need to throw tactics out the window and just come out swinging. For Nazi Germany and the Soviet Union, that happened in July 1943 outside the Russian city of Kursk. It was here, on a wide-open field decorated only with the occasional antitank trench or artillery gun, that the two most powerful land armies on earth fought the single-largest tank battle in human history.

It had been a long, hard, soul-suckingly terrible winter for the German Reich. After having their previously invincible army stopped at the gates of Moscow and then decisively kicked in the panzers in the frozen rubble of Stalingrad, the Nazi armies were now in the unfamiliar position of having to locate Reverse on their tanks' gearshifts. All across the Eastern Front, an almost endless wave of Soviet men and machines surged ahead, battering the Germans across a five-hundred-mile front.

But as the cold, mud-covered, frosty misery of the Russian

winter slowly melted away, the hardened veterans of the German Army knew it was time to drop another good old-fashioned blitzkrieg on the Russkies and turn this thing around once and for all. And this time, they had a secret weapon: the brand-spanking-new Tiger I heavy tank.

Of all the awesome tanks produced during World War II, none was more feared, more iconic, or deadlier than this one. The Tiger was a fifty-ton behemoth of steel with four-inch-thick armor plating and a super-intense 88mm main cannon. Streamrolling ahead at twenty-three miles per hour, this unstoppable, death-dealing Nazi monstrosity could blast apart Russian tanks from a mile away and then laugh while puny enemy antitank rounds pinged harmlessly off the hull with all the deadliness of a BB gun. Sure, they broke down a lot and the engine had a nasty habit of bursting into flames every so often. But when you can accurately launch a high-explosive bullet roughly the size of a golden retriever more than a mile while driving over a stone wall at twenty miles an hour, you tend to forgive that sort of thing.

So, in July 1943, equipped with a brand-new shipment of Tiger heavy tanks and equally dangerous Panther medium tanks, the Germans prepared to launch a massive counterattack that would sucker punch the Russkies and flip the table like a cranky dude who's just realized he's about to lose a ten-hour game of Monopoly. The plan, known as Operation Citadel, was your straight-up old-school German blitzkrieg

A Russian antitank crew at Kursk, 1943

pincer attack. This time it was aimed at trapping hundreds of thousands of Russian troops in a pocket outside the city of Kursk.

By this point in the war, the Russians had seen enough German pincer attacks to know what was up, and they did their best to build defenses accordingly. While the Germans waited for their trains to bring up enough Panther and Tiger tanks to mount an attack, the Russians put in minefields, built hundreds of hidden antitank guns, laid down miles of barbed wire, and dug trenches that were too wide and too deep for German tanks to cross. They knew where the attack was coming from and when it was happening.

But knowing the enemy plan and being able to stop it are two very different things.

A German tank at Kursk, 1943

Just before midnight on July 5, 1943, the Germans launched an all-out attack spearheaded in the south by the elite Second SS Panzer Corps and their ferocious Tiger and Panther tanks. A crushing wave of tanks, armored trucks, and other hulking war machines from the First, Second, and Third SS Panzer Divisions tore through the front lines of the Russian armies. Bunkers exploded into towering fireballs all down the line as German tanks trampled their way across the plains, and anything left standing was a target for the fleet of Luftwaffe bombers that blackened the skies above. Also there were the men and tanks of the Waffen-SS, handpicked for their stalwart devotion to Hitler and the Nazi Party and rocking the best training and weaponry in the Third Reich. Besides having impenetrable armor, better range, and a stronger gun than the Russian T-34s, these dudes were also veteran supersoldiers who could routinely get off two or three accurate shots from their main cannon in the time it took the Russian crews to fire once. In just seventeen hours, the Second SS Panzer Corps had advanced through the front lines of the Soviet defenses and were threatening to complete the encirclement and destruction of the Russian troops at Kursk.

The Russian commander, Marshal Georgy Zhukov, responded by deploying the entire First Guards Tank Army to meet the SS head-on.

Twenty-three-year-old Guard Lieutenant Aleksandra Samusenko was already a three-year veteran of the Red Army.

A T-34 tank knocked out at Kursk, 1943

Much of her background is clouded in mystery, but we do know that this dedicated woman had initially served in an infantry regiment during the Winter War with Finland in 1940. Because she had plenty of technical training as a mechanic, she was then sent to tank school in 1941 and trained on the T-34 medium battle tank. She'd fought Germans plenty of times and destroyed dozens of enemy antitank guns on the outskirts of Stalingrad. She was also wounded twice in battle, including one time when her tank was hit and caught fire and she barely escaped with her life. She'd earned the respect of her men so confidently that she was the only woman in the Red Army (and as of 2015, in any army in history) to command a tank on the battlefield. Directing a crew of three other tankers—a driver, a radioman, and a loader—it was her job to position the tank, lead the troops, and, oh yeah, fire the main cannon. Which is sweet.

With no air-conditioning, the crew of Samusenko's T-34 were baking in the July heat, but they just wiped the sweat from their foreheads and kept going. Slamming the control sticks forward (tanks use two control sticks, one for each tread, instead of a steering wheel), the driver gunned the 38.8-liter V-12 engine, rocking the thirty-ton, twenty-two-foot-long armored vehicle into action. An incredible 840 Soviet tanks hurtled through the wheat fields and grasslands, bearing down on 294 German tanks, including almost fifty of the dreaded Tigers. The Russians fired while on the

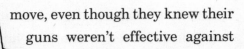

move, even though they knew their guns weren't effective against these new über-tanks at that range. Their only hope was to get in close as fast as possible. The Tigers took a fearsome toll, detonating T-34s and then rolling backward to keep their distance. All along the miles-long battlefield, the scene turned into a swirling melee of individual tank battles and general chaos. Tigers took out multiple T-34s, only to be destroyed by a Russian soldier running up and throwing a bomb in the window. T-34 "wolf packs" attacked other Tigers, swarming them in the hope that one of their own tanks could get a clear shot at the less-well-armored back end of the Tiger. Panzer IV tanks and T-34s went shot for shot with one another, and antitank guns and dive-bombers cratered the earth with humongous explosions.

In the middle of the battle, Aleksandra Samusenko suddenly found herself up against three Tigers from the Third SS Panzer Division. Telling her men "There is no turning back for us," she steeled her nerves and led her tank into battle, knowing that escape was not an option. Peering through the gunsights, she fired accurately and quickly, shooting on

the move to give the Tigers a more difficult target to hit. Somehow, with shells whirling around it, this lone T-34 was able to knock two of the enemy out of action with a couple of deadly accurate point-blank shots into the turrets of the enemy supertanks. Samusenko then damaged the third Tiger with a shell that forced it to withdraw. Later in the battle, her commanding officer was killed in action, and Samusenko took charge of the battalion and led them out of a firefight at point-blank range with Nazi panzers. For her accomplishments, she received the Order of the Red Star, a Soviet medal offered for exceptional leadership in combat. She was also promoted to captain and given command of the unit, making her the only woman in history ever to command a tank battalion.

Samusenko's immense bravery helped save her unit and took out a couple of enemy tanks in the process, but the First Guards Army would still be badly smashed up by the hardened SS panzers and would ultimately be forced back in tatters. However, they had done their job—they'd bought time for the Russians to redeploy troops to prevent a breakthrough. As Soviet IL-2 Sturmovik attack planes soared overhead, dropping bombs on the Germans, and swarms of tanks and men came surging into the battlefront from every direction, the Nazis realized they'd lost their opportunity for a quick, decisive blitzkrieg victory. The Germans would lose fifty thousand men and seven hundred tanks in the monthlong battle at Kursk, and by the time the dust settled, they were back in full retreat all across the Eastern Front.

It would be the last German attempt to counterattack the Russians in the war.

WHICH REICH WAS THAT AGAIN?

As I mentioned earlier, Nazi Germany is also known as the "Third Reich," with *Reich* being the German word for "kingdom" or "empire." The First Reich was the Holy Roman Empire, which began back in the Viking days with Charlemagne and ran until Napoleon dissolved it in 1806. The Second Reich was the German Empire of the Kaiser, which ran from the end of the Franco-Prussian War in 1871 until the German defeat in World War I.

DEATH FROM ABOVE

A brutal killer stalked the skies above the battlefront at Kursk: Hans-Ulrich Rudel, the most decorated serviceman in German military history and the most kill-crazy human being ever to fly an aircraft in combat. Piloting a Ju-87 Stuka dive-bomber, Rudel flew an obscene 2,530 combat missions in World War II, a number that dwarfs that of any pilot from any country ever. Between 1939 and 1945, he blew up 519 Soviet tanks, seventy amphibious boats, four armored trains, a cruiser, a destroyer, hundreds of trucks and armored vehicles, and even the Russian battleship *Murat*. Rudel also shot down eleven enemy airplanes. The guy was so successful that Hitler had to invent new bravery awards to give him.

SCHUTZSTAFFEL

The infamous and feared Schutzstaffel ("protective shield"), better known as the SS, was the name of the military arm of the Nazi Party. It's like if the Democrats or Republicans had an armed forces branch that reported to their politicians rather than to the US Army high command. The SS was initially created in 1925 as a small group of two hundred bodyguards, but once command was given to evil-looking, monocle-wearing Reichsführer-SS Heinrich Himmler, the sadistic organization took on a life of its own. By the time Germany attacked Poland, the SS consisted of something like 250,000 men. It was broken up into two groups: the Allgemeine-SS controlled the secret police (the Gestapo) and items related to "racial matters," while the Waffen-SS was made up of elite frontline military shock troops. These crazy scary guys were not considered part of the German Army and were under the direct control of Hitler himself (so was the army, I guess, but that's beside the point). SS divisions were composed almost exclusively of soldiers who could trace their Aryan lineage back three generations, and they were always given the best equipment, the best training, and the newest gear, making them by far the hardest-hitting forces in the German military.

HEROINES OF THE USSR

The Soviet Union was the only country in the war that allowed women to fight on the front lines, and the tales of their heroism are ones for the ages. Here are just a few of the many remarkable women who received the highest award for military bravery offered by the USSR, the title "Hero of the Soviet Union."

Lyudmila Pavlichenko

One of the toughest snipers of World War II, Lyudmila Pavlichenko was a student at Kiev State University who had been shooting rifles since she was fourteen years old. When the war began, she was trained as a nurse, but she grabbed a rifle at her first opportunity and immediately went to work shooting Nazis at long range. Eventually reclassified as a sniper, Pavlichenko battled through the rubble of cities and the wilderness of Eastern Europe, hunting down Nazis at every turn. This ironclad hellion is credited with taking out 309 enemy soldiers, including killing thirty-nine German snipers during the war. She was hit by a mortar shell outside Odessa in the Crimean Peninsula but recovered and spent the rest of the war as a teacher at Soviet sniper school.

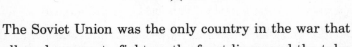

Lydia Litvyak

The "White Rose of Stalingrad," Lydia Litvyak had more air-to-air combat kills than any woman fighter ace in history. Going up against top-of-the-line German Messerschmitts in the bullet-riddled skies above Stalingrad, this daring woman went on sixty-six combat patrols and took out twelve enemy aircraft, making her a two-time fighter ace. On one mission, she shot down an eleven-kill German ace, who parachuted out of his burning aircraft and was eventually captured by the Soviets. He asked to meet the skillful pilot who had bested him, and when Litvyak approached, he was so impressed he offered her his gold watch. She calmly told him, "I do not accept gifts from my enemies." She was last seen in 1943, fighting heroically despite being attacked by eight enemy fighter planes at the same time.

Yekaterina Mikhaylova-Demina

Just sixteen years old when she volunteered for the Red Army, Yekaterina Mikhaylova-Demina was trained as a medic and assigned to work with the Russian marines. Working her way up to the rank of naval chief petty officer, Mikhaylova-Demina became famous across Russia for her actions during a daring midnight raid on German coastal positions in August 1944. With her platoon getting righteously shot up by enemy machine guns, this steely heroine personally saved the lives of seventeen men, then carried on the attack by herself and single-handedly took fourteen German soldiers prisoner. Four months after that, while attacking a fortress in Yugoslavia, she pulled seven wounded comrades out of icy water even though she'd already taken a bullet through her hand—one of the three wounds she'd receive during the war.

Mariya Oktyabrskaya

When this devoted wife's husband was killed in the fighting around Kiev in 1941, Mariya Oktyabrskaya sold her house and all her worldly possessions and used the money to buy a T-34 battle tank. Painting the phrase *Fighting Girlfriend* in those cool-looking Russian letters on the side of the turret, she hopped in, taught herself how to drive it, and then rolled it to the front lines to take her explosive vengeance. She offered to donate the tank to the Red Army, but only if she could be the driver, and she was set up with a crew from the Twenty-Sixth Guards Tank Brigade. Oktyabrskaya fearlessly drove her tank into battle at every opportunity, and, just in case you had any doubt about her enthusiasm, she also *got out of her tank in the middle of a firefight* after a German gun shot off one of her treads. She did this on three separate occasions before the Germans finally killed her.

Irina Sebrova

Flying a canvas-and-wood Polikarpov Po-2 biplane (one of those Red Baron–looking things with the double wings) that had been outdated since the 1920s, Flight Lieutenant Irina Sebrova undertook over a *thousand* attack missions against German bases during World War II. She was part of a unit known as the "Night Witches" that would wreak chaos and destruction on the Nazis in the middle of the night while they were trying to sleep. Because the plane was so old and noisy (the Russians used to refer to it as the "flying typewriter" because of the weird clanking noises it made), Sebrova would have to turn her plane off as she approached the enemy base, drop her bombs while in glide mode (!), then crank the engine back on and get out of there before she was blasted by antiaircraft guns. Sebrova was shot down twice during the war, which is a big deal because Night Witches weren't issued parachutes. But both times she survived the crash, evaded capture, and snuck her way back to the nearest Soviet base.

KNOW YOUR VEHICLES

	T-34/76	PzKpfw. VI Tiger
TYPE	Medium tank	Heavy tank
COUNTRY	Soviet Union	Germany
FIRST PRODUCED	1940	1943
LENGTH	21 feet, 11 inches	20 feet, 9 inches
WEIGHT	30 ton	50 tons
ARMOR	45 millimeters	100 millimeters
ENGINE	500-hp Model V-2-34 38.8L V-12	690-hp Maybach HL230 P45 V-12
TOP SPEED	32 mph	23 mph
CREW	4	5
ARMAMENT	One 76.2mm M-40 cannon Two 7.62mm machine guns	One 88mm KwK 36 L/5 Two 7.92mm machine guns

The German Tiger tank was bigger, stronger, and more heavily armored and packed a heavier gun, but the Soviet T-34 tank was way quicker and there were a LOT more of them. They were also a little less likely to break down and/or catch fire for no reason. The basic rule of thumb for Soviet tankers was that you needed three T-34s to take out one Tiger.

11

SOBIBOR

Escape from Hitler's Death Camp

Sobibor, Poland
October 14, 1943

We must get rid of the SS officers, and this should take one hour. If we could do it in less time, so much the better. For that purpose we need efficient and determined men, since one moment's hesitation would be fatal. I know some capable people who can do the job.

—Kapo Brzecki, Jewish prisoner at Sobibor

WHEN RED ARMY LIEUTENANT ALEXANDER Pechersky became a prisoner of war just ten days into Operation Barbarossa, he had no idea that his World War II nightmare was just beginning.

Before the Germans came rolling in and started breaking everything, "Sasha" Pechersky was a pretty average guy. He was a thirty-two-year-old bookkeeper and part-time composer who had written some cool piano and violin jams that were performed in his home village of Rostov-on-Don, Russia. He had a wife and a young daughter, worked hard, and led an ordinary existence that didn't involve fighting for his life or trying to kill Nazis with a hatchet.

Sasha Pechersky

All that changed in 1941, when the bookkeeper and amateur songwriter was conscripted into the Red Army to help fight off the German invasion of Russia.

Pechersky was given a uniform and a rifle and thrown into combat on the front lines as a basic infantry officer. He fought to defend his homeland for ten days, but when the blitzkrieg encircled and captured Minsk, his unit surrendered and he became a German prisoner of war.

Now, the Germans are pretty notorious for not being especially kind to their Russian prisoners of war (and vice versa), and for the next two years Lieutenant Pechersky endured a miserable existence imprisoned in a POW camp right in the middle of downtown Minsk. Food was scarce, brutal torment by the guards was commonplace, and the German SS camp commander had a nasty habit of letting his pet German shepherd attack people for no reason at all, shooting them if they hurt his poor little puppy. At one point, Pechersky caught typhus, a nasty disease carried by body lice; it gives you a fever, muscle pain, sensitivity to light, and vomiting. Since typhus was a death sentence for Russian POWs (the Germans would rather just shoot you and burn your body than give you any kind of medicine), Pechersky somehow kept this condition a secret for over a week in order to survive.

The Russian lieutenant was certain things couldn't get much worse.

He was wrong.

In 1943 it became known to the SS that Sasha Pechersky was Jewish. He, along with two thousand other Jewish Red Army prisoners of war, was ordered to cram himself onto a long train, where he spent the next ninety-six hours crossing Eastern Europe in a sweltering cattle car packed so tight nobody could even sit down.

On September 23, 1943, he arrived at Sobibor extermination camp.

Adolf Hitler and the Nazi Party had come to power in Germany on a political platform of hating the Jews. Persecution of Jewish people under the Third Reich began as early as 1933, when Hitler stripped every single person with at least one Jewish grandparent of all their wealth and citizenship, herded them into ghettos, and gave them just enough food to still pretty much starve to death. This wasn't killing

Jewish detainees boarding trains to Treblinka extermination camp, 1942

people fast enough for Hitler, though, so in January 1942 he authorized the Final Solution to the Jewish Question: the construction of elaborate death camps designed to systematically exterminate all Jews on earth.

Sobibor was one of those camps.

It's beyond the scope of this book to get too deeply into the horrors of the Holocaust, but let's just say it was almost certainly the worst thing that has ever happened in the history of humanity. If you'd like to know more about it, ask a teacher or librarian for books and other resource recommendations. Of the two thousand POWs who arrived at Sobibor, Pechersky was one of just eighty strong-looking, able-bodied men and women chosen to work as slave laborers for the German war effort. The rest were sent to a showerlike facility and executed by poison gas, which was deployed through the ventilation system. Their bodies were then cremated to conceal any evidence of what was going on. An estimated 250,000 people were killed in this way at Sobibor, just a percentage of the six million Jewish men, women, and children who perished during the Holocaust.

Sasha Pechersky knew he had to escape by any means necessary, and he had to give everyone else the chance to get free, too.

It wouldn't be easy. The prisoners at Sobibor were exhausted, overworked, and starving, and the facility itself was locked up like a fortress. There had been an uprising at the Treblinka death camp a few weeks earlier that had set a few buildings on fire, so it was certainly possible, but in the aftermath of that escape, the Nazis had stepped up their defenses.

Sobibor was about a half mile from end to end and was home to about six hundred POWs, plus thirty Nazi SS officers and between 90 and 120 Ukrainian or Polish volunteer guardsmen. It was surrounded by three rows of barbed wire, an electrified fence, a deep antitank trench, and a

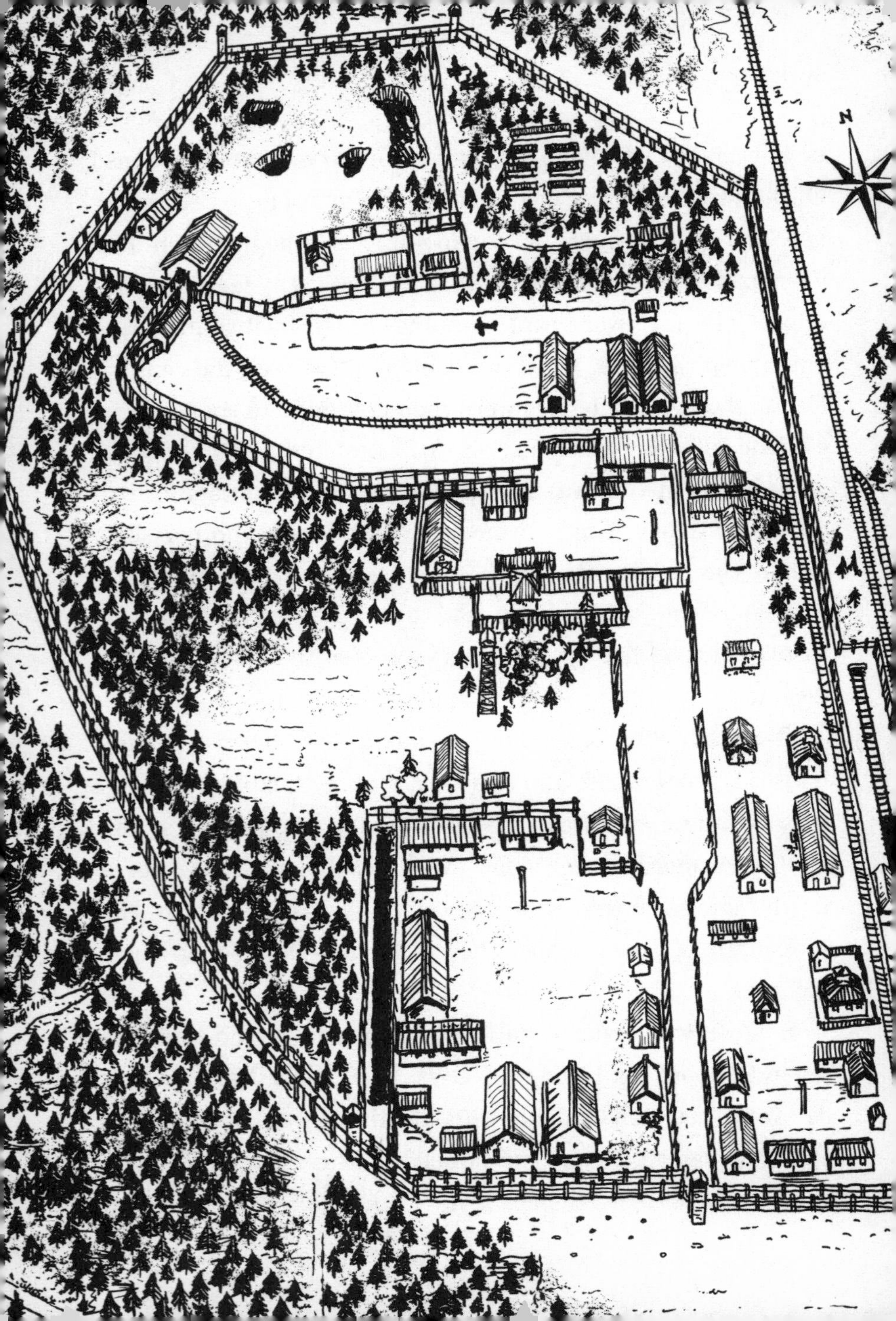
N

fifty-foot-wide minefield. Watchtowers placed every couple hundred feet were equipped with fearsome MG34 machine guns. Worse yet, the SS made it very clear that any attempt to escape, even by one person, would result in mass shootings of prisoners.

Not long after arriving, Pechersky met up with a Polish tailor named Leon Feldhendler, and together they secretly began planning to break out while they still had the strength to do it. First they dug a tunnel, but it didn't work out—heavy rain turned the dirt to mud and it collapsed. So they opted to go the more direct route, which was to kill every SS officer in the camp and walk right out the front door.

The cabinetmakers' workshop was the perfect hub for their plotting. It was quiet, it had places to hide things, and the second floor offered a good view of the camp so they could watch for guards and plan strategies. Plus, it wasn't weird for a bunch of people to congregate in there, and it kept the guards' suspicions down. The Nazis had many terrible ways of beating information out of you, and if just one person coughed up the details of the plot, it would mean death for everyone involved.

Over the next few weeks, people from across the camp worked together to prepare for the uprising. Women in the SS offices snuck out grenades, ammo, and a pistol. Blacksmiths secretly forged small knives or smuggled out wire cutters and hatchets. Other observers documented guards' schedules or approached potential collaborators to join the cause.

Finally, on October 14, 1943, the plan was ready to be put into action. Feldhendler, the tailor, set up fittings for new uniforms for the SS officers. Other craftsmen said that new shoes were ready, or asked SS guys for help looking at a new weapon belt, or whatever—anything they could to lure these guys out of the open and into a quiet, closed-in workshop, where other prisoners could ambush them with knives and hatchets. All across the camp, no fewer than ten SS officers (including the acting camp commander) were secretly and quietly taken out, their bodies hidden, and the blood covered up with sawdust.

Now was the time to move.

Pechersky's men cut the telephone wires and the power

to the electrified fence, then lined up as if they were a work detail and headed out for the fence. Just as they were about to get there, they pulled the pistols they'd taken from the dead officers and opened fire, while other prisoners gave a huge yell and rushed ahead with knives and axes.

It was anarchy. As the leaderless camp guards struggled to react, inmates stormed the weapons arsenal, cut through barbed wire, or simply made a break out the front gates toward the forest beyond. They killed guards with their bare hands or with pistols, scaled walls, and ripped up barbed wire. Machine-gun fire from a half dozen towers raked the unarmed prisoners as they ran for it, but Pechersky and others who had found rifles did what they could to silence them with accurate gunfire. Many determined escapees were hit by rifle fire or machine-gun fire, and still more were killed while trying to run across the minefield, but all across the camp perimeter, fleeing prisoners miraculously reached the relative safety of the forest. Of the six hundred people interned in Sobibor, nearly four hundred made it out. They left behind ten dead SS officers and thirty-eight dead camp guards. An additional thirty guards simply deserted their posts and ran for it.

Lieutenant Sasha Pechersky, the bookkeeper turned guerrilla leader, was with a group of about sixty guys who cut through the barbed wire and reached the forest. As the Germans were certainly going to bring up reinforcements to track down the escaped prisoners, Sasha made the decision to split into smaller groups to try to escape the Nazi dragnet. He and a few other folks reached a nearby Polish village, where some kind locals gave them food and water and information about the best escape routes.

For nine harrowing days, Pechersky and his small band made their way through the unfamiliar forests of Poland, hiding during the day and moving under cover of darkness, all the while avoiding German patrols and living off the land for food and water. Finally, after an exhausting trip, they were able to link up with a group of Jewish partisans who were fighting an underground war against the German occupation. Sasha's skills as an infantry officer and his obvious resourcefulness were a perfect fit, and he joined immediately.

For the last two years of the war, Lieutenant Pechersky fought as a guerrilla warrior, derailing Nazi trains, setting mines on railroad tracks, blowing up bridges, and bombing enemy barracks. He led hit-and-run raids on supply depots, attacked convoys, and did whatever he could to wreak havoc on the enemy and to make them pay for what they'd done. After the war, a street was named after him in Israel, and he testified at the war crimes trials of twelve Nazi officers—ten of whom were hanged for crimes against humanity.

Of the four hundred escapees from the Sobibor uprising, roughly half were tracked down and killed by the SS. The rest went into hiding, joined guerrilla outfits, or simply disappeared. After the disaster at the death camp, SS commander Heinrich

Himmler ordered the camp shut down and the entire complex demolished. Every building and watchtower was blown up, and all the bodies and poison gas were destroyed. While many other Nazi death camps stayed in operation right up until the very end of the war, Sobibor was never used again.

THE AUSCHWITZ REVOLT

The most brutal of the Holocaust death camps was Auschwitz, where over a million people were systematically executed. This heavily fortified execution camp was virtually escape proof, but a woman named Rosa Robota and other Jewish prisoners working in the camp's crematorium were able to smuggle in bombs, blow up one of the buildings, and incite an uprising against the guards. Several SS agents were killed in the struggle, but ultimately the revolt failed and the reprisals were brutal. Rosa was slowly tortured to death by the SS over the course of several weeks but never revealed the names of her co-conspirators. After the war, Polish courts would hunt down many of the men responsible for the camp and sentence them to death by hanging.

HORRORS OF WAR

Between military and civilian casualties, the Soviet Union suffered over twenty million casualties throughout the course of World War II. This number is larger than the present-day populations of each of these countries: Chile, the Netherlands, Greece, Portugal, and the Czech Republic. Poland suffered just as catastrophically—in the Warsaw Ghetto alone, over seven hundred thousand civilians died of starvation, dehydration, or illness, or were simply shot in the streets by the Nazis. That number is greater than the number of battle casualties sustained by the entire United States Armed Forces over the course of World War II.

European Jewish Population

1939	1945
9,500,000	3,800,000

12

VOYTEK THE SOLDIER BEAR

Polish II Corps and the Battle for Monte Cassino

Monte Cassino, Italy
May 18, 1944

He liked a cigarette, he liked a bottle of beer—he drank a bottle of beer like any man.

—Augustyn Karolewski, Polish First Armored Division

IN **1943** POLISH SOLDIERS TRAINED AN ADULT brown bear to help them fight Nazis in an old monastery atop a mountain in the Italian Alps.

Yes, this is a true story, not the plot of the next Pixar film. The bear doesn't sing or dance or talk, but it does carry artillery shells, take baths, and smoke cigarettes, even though smoking is really bad for you.

Voytek the Soldier Bear's story starts back during the German blitzkrieg against Poland at the very beginning of the war. As the Nazis were crushing their way through western Poland, the brave Polish defenders suddenly felt the stab of a knife in their back when the forces of the Soviet Union came rolling across Poland's eastern border, eager to grab land for the USSR while the Polish were preoccupied with getting punched in the head by the German Army.

One of the few, outnumbered defenders who stood his ground against the Soviet juggernaut was Captain Wladislaw Anders, a resolute cavalry officer who valiantly launched a charge against Soviet troops but was wounded in battle and taken as a prisoner of war. For over a year he rotted in Lubyanka Prison, one of Stalin's worst and most inhospitable one-star prison facilities.

Then a weird thing happened. On August 14, 1941, the Red Army guards unlocked the prison cell and told Anders he was a free man. The Germans had invaded Russia, and now the Soviets were prepared to offer Anders and 1.5 million other Polish citizens their freedom if they'd help old Uncle Joe Stalin battle those big evil Nazis.

Anders cocked an eyebrow. He wasn't exactly crazy about the idea of trusting his life to the men who had just shot and imprisoned him, but he agreed anyway. He was shipped out by rail and reunited with twenty-five thousand other Polish soldiers who had been similarly released from the Soviet prison system. Anders immediately led them out of the country, taking them by rail south into Iran so they could link up with the British Commonwealth Army there (more on the Commonwealth at the end of the chapter).

It was a smart move.

The British reorganized "Anders's Army," dubbing it Polish II Corps. After a brief time rearming, training, and gearing up, the Poles shipped off toward Palestine so they could take part in the Allied invasion of Italy.

While traveling through Iran with the British, the men of the Polish II Corps's Twenty-Second Transport Artillery Supply Company came across a young Iranian boy wandering through the desert, carrying a large cloth sack. The men thought the boy looked tired and hungry, so they gave him some food. When the kid thanked them, the Poles asked what was in the bag. The boy opened it up and revealed a tiny, malnourished brown bear cub. Since the soldiers knew the little cub was in very poor health and needed attention quickly, they bought the bear from the kid and fed it some condensed milk from a makeshift bottle. For the next several days, they nursed the bear back to health, giving it food, water, and a warm place to sleep.

Over the long journey from Iran to Palestine, the bear, now named Voytek (it's spelled *Wojtek* in Polish but pronounced

"Voytek" because Polish is a funny language like that), quickly became the unofficial mascot of the Twenty-Second Company. The bear would sit around the campfire with the men, eating, drinking, and sleeping in tents with the rest of the soldiers. He loved smoking and eating cigarettes, drank beer right out of the bottle like a regular infantryman, and got a kick out of wrestling and play-fighting. Of course, he was the best wrestler in the entire company, thanks in part to the fact that he grew to be six feet tall, weighed roughly five hundred pounds, and could knock small trees over with a single swing of his big, adorable clawed paw. He improved the morale of men who were fighting without a home to go back to, and he was treated as though he were just another hard-drinkin', hard-smokin', hard-fightin', hair-growin' soldier in the company. When the unit marched out on a mission, Voytek would stand up on his hind legs and march alongside them. When the motorized convoy was on the move, Voytek sat in the passenger seat of one of the jeeps, hanging his head out

Polish troops wrestling with Voytek

the window and drawing plenty of looks from people walking down the street.

For some reason Voytek also enjoyed taking hot showers. Over the summer in Palestine, he learned how to work the showers, and you could pretty much always find him splashing around the bathhouse. Once, he entered the bathhouse and came across a spy who had been planted to gather intelligence on the Allied camp. Voytek growled, slapped the dude upside his head, and then stood there staring at him until the guy surrendered and confessed to being an Axis spy. He was interrogated and gave up valuable intelligence on enemy movements.

After passing through Egypt, Polish II Corps linked up with Montgomery's British Eighth Army and prepared to

deploy in the Italian invasion. The problem, however, was that British High Command did not allow any pets or other animals in their camp, so the Polish Army formally enlisted Voytek the Bear into their ranks. He was given the rank of private, was assigned a serial number, and from that point on was included in all official unit rosters. The Brits were like, "Whatever, chaps," and didn't even bat an eye when Voytek marched ashore with the rest of the Twenty-Second Company.

The Poles' finest hour of the war came during the incredibly bloody battle for Monte Cassino (a mountain in Italy) in May 1944. By the time Polish II Corps arrived, the elite German soldiers of the First Parachute Division were firmly entrenched in the ruins of a sixth-century Benedictine monastery, high at the top of the seventeen-hundred-foot-tall mountain. Fighting in driving rain and thick mud, the Allies had launched four previous attacks up the mountain toward the monastery, but sniper fire and machine guns had turned them back with grievous casualties every single time. The campaign was proving to be one of the bloodiest battles of the Western Front, and the Poles were brought in to make the final push to capture the fortress.

During the fighting, Voytek the Hero Bear actually hand-carried boxes of ammunition, some weighing in at over a hundred pounds, to artillery positions on the front lines. You have to assume that it was pretty demoralizing to the

Germans to see that the Poles had a giant bear fighting on their side. Voytek worked tirelessly, day and night, bringing supplies to his friends who were bravely battling the Nazis. He never rested, never dropped a single artillery shell, and never showed any fear despite being under constant enemy fire and heavy shelling. His actions were so inspiring to his fellow soldiers that after the battle the official insignia of the Twenty-Second Artillery Supply Company was changed to a picture of Voytek carrying an armful of high-explosive artillery ammunition.

Thanks in part to the heavy shelling by their artillery, the Polish forces attacked in the middle of the night, broke through the Nazi defenses, and captured Monte Cassino, although they lost over four thousand men. They raised Polish and British flags high atop the mountain on May 18, and within two weeks the road to Rome had been blown open.

Voytek and his comrades went on to fight the Germans across the Italian peninsula, breaking through the enemy lines, slamming into the heavily defended Italian-German border, and forcing back three of the best divisions in the German Wehrmacht. After the war, some elements of the Polish Army, including Voytek, were reassigned to Scotland, since Poland was under the control of the USSR and many of the soldiers feared they would be arrested for deserting the Soviet army. Voytek lived out the rest of his days in the

Edinburgh Zoo, where he died in 1963 at the age of twenty-two. It was said that he always perked up when he heard the Polish language spoken by zoo guests, and during his life there he was often visited by his old friends from the Polish Army—some of whom would throw cigarettes down into his open arms or even jump into the enclosure and wrestle with him for old times' sake.

Voytek the bear, 1942

HAVE FUN STORMING THE CASTLE

Elsewhere on the Italian boot, Lieutenant Vernon J. Baker fought his way through an intense battle high in the Italian Alps. Commanding a twenty-five-man machine-gun platoon from the all-African-American Ninety-Second Infantry Division, Baker was ordered to assault a heavily fortified Italian castle that was garrisoned by dozens of German troops. Baker led his team through dense forested mountainsides to within 250 yards of the imposing mountain fortress, personally cleared out two German bunkers Solid Snake style without making a sound, then cut the fortress's phone lines and led the attack. He and his men fought hard but were pinned down in an olive grove outside the fortress. With only six men left in his unit, Baker jumped up and drew enemy fire so the rest of his team could escape. Once they were on their way to safety, he went nuts with his machine gun, single-handedly wiping out six machine-gun nests, two observation posts, and four enemy dugouts despite being shot twice during the fighting. He survived, returned to base, came back the next night with fresh troops from a different unit, and captured the castle. Lieutenant Baker received the Medal of Honor, and his final assault on the Italian fortress marked one of the first times in US history when a black soldier commanded white soldiers in combat.

ANDERS'S ARMY

The nonbear members of Polish II Corps occupied Italy after the war, where they were joined by other Poles who had escaped from oppression at the hands of either the Germans or the Soviets. After the occupation, the 114,000 still-homeless Poles (Poland remained in Soviet control even after the war) would head back to England as part of the Polish Resettlement Corps, where they were given English-language classes and taught a profession. Anders, despite being a national hero, had his Polish citizenship stripped by the Soviet-controlled government of Poland in 1946 for "conduct detrimental to the country." He knew the truth, though, as did all his grateful soldiers.

THE COMMONWEALTH

For folks outside the United Kingdom, the highly complicated idea of the British Commonwealth can be even more confusing than when British people refer to soccer as "football." It would take six volumes to explain the Commonwealth in detail, but here's the short version: At the start of World War II, the United Kingdom (a.k.a. Great Britain) was made up of England, Scotland, Wales, and Northern Ireland. Each of those places had its own parliament, kind of the way US states have their own governors and legislatures. But *everything* was run by the British Parliament, a group of politicians led by the prime minister (at the time, it was Winston Churchill). There was also a monarch (King George VI), who was technically the numero uno main head honcho in charge of the whole United Kingdom enchilada. But in reality the monarch just went along with whatever Parliament wanted to do. Outside the United Kingdom were countries known as dominions: Canada, Newfoundland, Australia, New Zealand, South Africa, and Eire (formerly the Irish Free State). These were independent countries with their own governments, but George VI was also *their* king, and if he was at war with someone, then they pretty much were as well. (However, Eire remained neutral during World War II.) Then we get to India, where the people wanted to have their own country (but didn't get it until 1947) and were led by a viceroy—a British guy who reported to the British Parliament and basically told the Indians what to do all the time. It was a similar situation in the colonies, British-controlled lands that included Jamaica and Hong Kong. There were also mandates, such as Palestine and Iraq, and protectorates, such as Egypt and Sudan, but all of it really just boiled down to one thing: At the time of World War II, the British Commonwealth covered one-quarter of the planet, with territory on six continents, and it could call on hundreds of millions of soldiers to help fight against the forces of Hitler.

POP CULTURE IN 1942

One of the cool things about our current era is that it's one of the first times in history when modern folks can get on a computer and listen to the same things people were listening to during World War II. Sure, you can stream a Churchill or a Roosevelt speech, but you can also hear some of the most popular tunes. Cole Porter, the Ink Spots, Frank Sinatra, Ella Fitzgerald, and Glenn Miller were favorites, as was jazz music performed by Duke Ellington and Louis Armstrong. The bestselling song in America at the time of D-Day was Bing Crosby's "I Love You." The Mills Brothers' "Paper Doll" was number one for twelve weeks during 1943 and 1944. The patriotic song "God Bless America" had just been written in 1938, but President Roosevelt confessed that his favorite song was "Home on the Range."

Josef Stalin's favorite song was Sulkhan Tsintsadze's arrangement of "Suliko," and because everyone was afraid of Stalin, it got played on the radio in Moscow, like, all the time. Another popular song was "Katyusha," a ditty about a girl missing her soldier boyfriend. It was so popular with the troops that they named a rocket launcher truck after it.

The Germans were also into playing patriotic tunes,

as well as Hitler speeches and works by German composers like Beethoven and Wagner. However, the most popular song in Nazi Germany was "Lili Marlene." The tune was played so regularly that the British code breakers picked it up while they were scanning German radio frequencies. They liked the song and translated it into English, and it became a big hit in the UK.

A television was still a super-rare piece of equipment in the 1940s, but pretty much every single house in America and Europe had a radio of some kind sitting in the living room. The center of entertainment for most folks, the radio broadcast live-action shows, news, political propaganda, and music directly to the homes of people across the world. If you wanted to watch something, you had to go to the movie theater. The biggest movie stars at the time were guys like Clark Gable, Cary Grant, James Cagney, Henry Fonda, and Laurence Olivier, and leading ladies like Bette Davis, Ginger Rogers, Joan Fontaine, Ingrid Bergman, and Barbara Stanwyck. Popular movies were 1941's *Citizen Kane*, *Sergeant York*, and *The Maltese Falcon*, and in 1942 Humphrey Bogart stole the show with *Casablanca*. Disney cartoon movies like *Pinocchio*, *Fantasia*, *Dumbo*, and *Bambi* all came out between 1940 and 1942 and are still popular today. For action heroes, the big names were Errol Flynn and Gary Cooper, and audiences also flocked to watch beautiful women like Rita Hayworth, Lana Turner, Betty Grable, Jane Russell,

Judy Garland, and Hedy Lamarr. Incidentally, Hedy Lamarr was an Austrian who escaped her Nazi husband in the 1930s, fled to the United States, invented a type of wireless communication device used by the army during the war, and then went on to star in a bunch of successful movies. Alfred Hitchcock was just getting started in the business, while classic old-school monster movie heroes like Bela Lugosi, Lon Chaney Jr., and Boris Karloff were at the downside of their careers and stuck doing things like *Frankenstein Meets the Wolf Man.* For comedy, audiences cracked up while watching Abbott and Costello and the Three Stooges.

KNOW YOUR VEHICLES

	North American P-51D Mustang	Messerschmitt Me-262
TYPE	Long-range escort fighter plane	Jet fighter-interceptor aircraft
COUNTRY	United States	Germany
FIRST PRODUCED	1944	1944
LENGTH	32 feet, 3 inches	34 feet, 9 inches
WEIGHT	9,200 pounds	14,272 pounds
ENGINE	1,490-hp Packard V-1650-7 supercharged V-12	Two Junkers Jumo 004 B-1 turbojets
TOP SPEED	437 mph	559 mph
RATE OF CLIMB	3,200 feet per minute	3,900 feet per minute
CREW	1	1
ARMAMENT	Six .50-caliber machine guns Six T64 5-inch rockets Up to 2,000 pounds of bombs	Four 30mm autocannons Six T64 5-inch rockets Twenty-four 55mm R4M rockets Two 550-pound bombs

Near the end of 1944, Allied pilots encountered a dangerous new enemy: the Me-262, the world's first jet fighter. There weren't many of these newfangled jet aircraft in existence yet, and the Americans battled them heroically, destroying several. But the US planes were completely outclassed by this new breed. During the war, German Me-262 pilots claimed over five hundred Allied aircraft kills.

13

THE MIGHTY EIGHTH

The Flight of Cabin in the Sky III

February 20, 1944
Leipzig, Germany

Hitler built a fortress around Europe, but he forgot to put a roof on it.

—US president Franklin D. Roosevelt

"BANDITS, INCOMING, THREE O'CLOCK HIGH!" The sudden thumping of twelve machine guns all blasting at once jolted the fifteen-ton, four-engine aircraft, but United States Army Air Force Lieutenant William R. Lawley Jr. held it steady. The rumbling propellers roared as he pushed open the throttle and careened through a thick black cloud of antiaircraft smoke at nearly three hundred miles an hour. He had to keep in tight formation with hundreds of other gigantic, explosives-filled aircraft that were roughly the same size as those 737 airliners you see at the airport these days.

Overhead, a pair of ultrafast Nazi Focke-Wulf 190 fighter planes zoomed by, ripping off thousands of rounds from twin-linked machine guns and heavy autocannons. White tracer fire whizzed past the cockpit, while other bullets punched holes through the sides of the plane with the unsettling ping of steel on steel. Black puffs of enemy artillery popped up all around Lawley's massive aircraft, each one representing a ship-incinerating surface-to-air artillery shell bursting into a fearsome-looking cloud of screaming-hot shrapnel. The enemy fighters whipped past at speeds of over four hundred miles an hour, passing so close to Lawley's windshield that if he hadn't been so busy trying to keep his crew alive he probably could have told you the color of the pilots' eyes. As the gray Nazi fighters dove down toward another squadron of American bombers below, Lawley's starboard waist gunner zeroed in on them with a quick burst of tracer fire from his .50-caliber machine gun, but he had to release the trigger as a pair of American P-47 Thunderbolt fighter planes dropped in to chase them.

It was February 20, 1944, and Lieutenant Lawley's Boeing B-17 Flying Fortress was at the head of a formation of one thousand bombers sent to flatten Germany's production and aircraft manufacturing facilities into smoldering rubble. For

B-17 bombers in formation

some strange reason, the Germans were doing their best to make it difficult for the Americans to do this.

In early 1944, Nazi Germany was still reeling from the grinding defeat at the Battle of Kursk and was now being forced back all along the Eastern Front. The Allies were like, "Okay, cool, this is great and all, but total victory over Hitler's goose-stepping minions means a war on two fronts." This meant that at some point there would have to be a joint American-British full-scale invasion of Europe through France to squeeze out Hitler's forces, but that was easier said than done. Hitler had spent the last four years turning the entire French coastline into his so-called "Fortress Europe," bristling with cannons and aircraft from Calais to the Pyrenees. Much the way the Luftwaffe had needed to take out Britain's air defenses to mount a successful invasion of the British Isles, now the Allies needed to plaster the German military with a few million tons of high explosives and grind it into ash before attempting a full-blown attack into France.

The cleverly nicknamed "Big Week" was the Allied plan to spend seven days ruthlessly airmailing explosives to enemy aircraft-production facilities. Day and night, wave after wave of American B-17 Flying Fortresses, B-24 Liberators, and British Lancasters blasted shipyards, railroad junctions, power plants, airfields, steel-production facilities, dams, and military bases. They ignited everything from ball bearing plants to oil refineries, turning them into towering, explosive fireballs and making it really, really hard for anyone in Germany to build a working fighter plane.

These gigantic bomber raids were nothing new for Lieutenant Lawley. A twenty-three-year-old Alabama boy, this veteran pilot had already flown nine missions over Germany in the last year, running through a brutal gauntlet of antiaircraft cannons and enemy fighter planes every single time. This was his tenth mission, but his first at the controls of a brand-new B-17. It was nicknamed *Cabin in the Sky III* because the first two *Cabin in the Sky* aircraft under Lawley's command had already been blown up. (As a side note, *Cabin* was named after a musical that marked the first on-screen appearance of the moonwalk dance that Michael Jackson made so famous in the eighties, a fact that contributes very little to World War II history but is still cool.)

Lawley's target was an aircraft-production plant in Leipzig, a German fortress city just two hours from downtown Berlin. The Nazis, fighting on their own turf, were determined to stop Lawley and his buddies from pulverizing them.

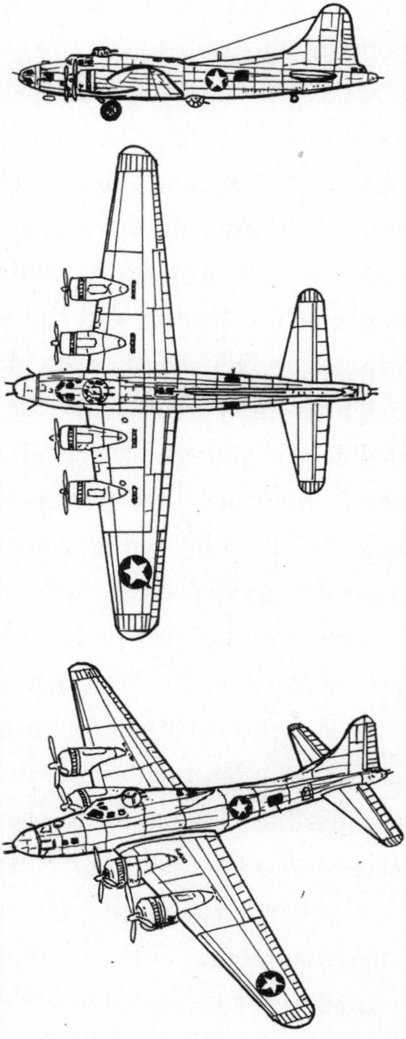

Flying Fortress wasn't just a clever name for the Boeing B-17 bomber. This behemoth was a four-engine, eighteen-ton armored tank with wings and enough machine guns to carve a small mountain into something resembling a giant chunk of Swiss cheese. It had a crew of ten: Pilot, copilot, flight engineer, navigator, bombardier, and radioman all worked together to bring the plane into position and release the bombs, and then there were four guys assigned as machine gunners. The ball turret gunner sat in the "suicide seat," a cramped little circular dome popping out from under the airplane that looked like those plastic balls you see at a McDonald's PlayPlace. It sported twin .50-caliber machine guns and swiveled a full 360 degrees. The tail gunner wedged himself into a tiny compartment in the back of the aircraft and was responsible for taking out enemy fighters that dropped in behind the B-17. There were also two machine gunners in the waist of the plane, each manning a gun facing a different side. Add a top-mounted double-machine-gun turret for the flight engineer and a front-facing double-machine-gun turret sticking out below the cockpit for the bombardier, then pack everything into an armored hull capable of withstanding extreme punishment from enemy aircraft and you've got, well, a flying fortress.

Over four hundred of these bombers partied above Leipzig as the B-17s of the American Eighth Air Force made their attack run. Peering through their mostly accurate state-of-the-art Norden bombsights and updating their calculations, bombardiers zeroed in on their targets and let fly, sending thousands of pounds of high explosives plummeting five miles to the earth to explode in a carpet of flame and shrapnel. In his rumbling cockpit, braving temperatures running to minus fifty degrees Fahrenheit, Lieutenant Lawley breathed

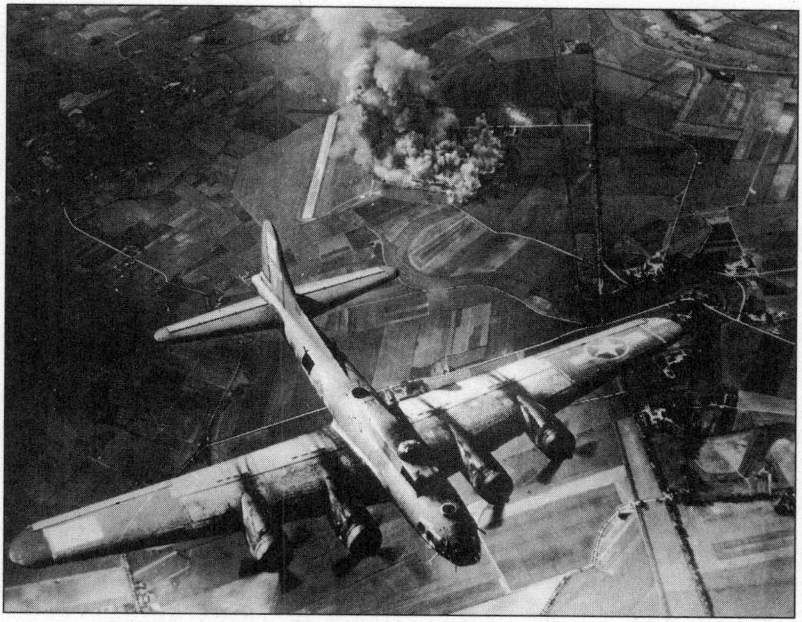

The US Eighth Air Force striking the Focke-Wulf plant in Marienburg, Poland

oxygen through a gas mask, because this was back before cool things like pressurized, heated aircraft existed. Holding the plane perfectly steady to give his bombardier a stable firing platform was risky because it made Lawley's B-17 a pretty cherry target for German ground gunners, but that was one of the risks they had to take.

Bomb explosions rippled the German countryside like a handful of rocks thrown into a lake, each pop representing a leveled building or factory. But on *Cabin in the Sky* there was a problem—the bomb doors wouldn't open. Ice from the extremely cold temperatures at the plane's high altitude had frozen the bomb racks in place, and they didn't deploy with the rest of the bombs from other American planes. So as the rest of the B-17s accelerated forward, relieved of their heavy bomb loads, *Cabin in the Sky* lagged slightly behind. Lawley opened the throttle to try to compensate.

Suddenly voices on *Cabin in the Sky*'s intercom called out another formation of Focke-Wulfs, this time diving down from behind. With the sun at their backs, blinding the tail gunner, the Focke-Wulfs ignored the deadly clouds of flak whomping apart the sky around them and hurtled straight into the B-17 formation. Their 20mm cannons struck home at one nearby American bomber, catching its engines on fire and ungracefully dropping it out of the sky like a brick trailing a black cloud of smoke and flame.

Another flak explosion hit even closer, rocking *Cabin in the Sky* and peppering one of the engines with shards of metal, causing it to burst into flames. Lawley ordered the copilot to shut it down and kept moving.

More calls came in. Six o'clock low. Three o'clock level. The Nazis were everywhere. The B-17s stuck close together like a herd of bison, knowing that the only way to survive was to stay close and lay down heavy fields of machine-gun fire.

As his gunners fired in every direction, Lawley looked through his cockpit window to see a fleet of twenty or so 190s drop down in front of him, pick out targets, and open fire.

With a deafening crash, a 20mm high-explosive autocannon shell burst through the front window of *Cabin in the Sky*, exploding in the cockpit. Everything went black.

Lawley snapped awake seconds later, his ears ringing as if he'd been inside a church bell when it was pulled. Alarms were going off all across his console, which was now decorated with shards of shrapnel. Through blurry vision, Lawley saw his copilot slumped over dead, his body lying on the control stick, pushing it forward. The plane was in a steep dive, made all the worse by the fact that it still had loaded bomb racks. The pilot-side window was smashed, and broken glass had gone into Lawley's face, arms, and side. The windshield was so smeared with blood and oil that he could barely see out of it. Another engine was on fire.

Amazingly, Lieutenant William Lawley didn't panic.

He did his job.

Determined to keep his plane and his crew alive, the veteran USAAF pilot reached out with his right arm, grabbed his dead copilot, and somehow pulled him back off the controls. Then, with just his left hand, Lawley manually fought a twenty-seven-ton bomber aircraft out of a ninety-degree nose-first dive at twelve thousand feet, leveled it off, and shut down the second burning engine. Looking up, he saw the Focke-Wulf pilots circling around for another pass, so this grim warrior made an evasive turn, dove the plane down into the cloud cover, and accelerated out of there as fast as he could.

Other B-17s in the formation had radioed *Cabin in the Sky* as "killed in action," but somehow William Lawley managed to evade the enemy fighters and get the heck out of Leipzig. He flew across Germany, dodging enemy AA positions, then flew in low over the French countryside and ordered the surviving eight members of his crew to grab parachutes and bail out.

Unfortunately, all eight crewmen had been wounded in the attack, and two of them were hurt so badly they couldn't possibly go skydiving right now. Nobody jumped out of the plane.

The bombardier eventually got the racks unstuck and released his bombs over an unimportant part of the French countryside, but before long another squadron of Me-109 fighters picked up the wounded B-17 on radar and came swooping in for the kill. With his injured guys moving to their guns to spray .50-caliber machine-gun fire, Lawley hammered the stick of his crippled plane, dodging and evading with one arm and somehow eluding the enemy fighters again. In the process, however, he had to use more fuel than he'd have liked, and one of the two remaining engines was now almost out of gas.

Despite Lawley's briefly passing out from lack of blood and then being revived by his bombardier, *Cabin in the Sky* somehow reached the English Channel against all odds, received emergency landing permission from a Canadian fighter base on the English coast, and, just in case you're wondering how this could possibly get any worse, when William Lawley hit the button to drop his landing gear wheels—you guessed it—they didn't deploy.

So, limping in with three burned-out engines and "feathering" his only working one by pumping it off and on with small amounts of gas, Lieutenant William Lawley—who was half blinded by broken glass, was exhausted from loss of blood, and had no landing gear, eight wounded crew members, and one good arm—attempted to crash-land an eighteen-ton Flying Fortress on a grass airfield about the size of a soccer field.

He came in hard on his belly, sliding across the airfield, finally coming to a rest just outside the Canadian barracks. Every remaining member of his crew survived.

Lawley would walk out of the wreckage, spend a few weeks in the hospital, and make a full recovery. He went on to successfully pilot four more bombing missions before the war was over.

BOMBER KILLERS

One of the leading Luftwaffe antibomber pilots was Hermann Staiger, an Me-109 pilot who had custom-upgraded his plane with an aircraft-demolishing 30mm autocannon. Staiger had shot down a Spitfire over Dunkirk, recorded seven kills during the Battle of Britain, and took out three Soviet bombers on the first day of Operation Barbarossa. But he was wounded by antiaircraft fire shortly after and had to return to Germany to recuperate. Staiger later flew his Me-109 to wreak havoc on the Eighth Air Force. This fearless pilot once took out five B-17s in a single day and recorded a total of sixty-three air-to-air kills during the war—including twenty-six heavy bombers.

BUILT FORD TOUGH

B-17 Flying Fortresses were produced by Boeing, the same company that produces commercial airliners. All across the world, corporations—especially car companies—switched over their manufacturing plants to help the war efforts. Buick plants produced seventy-five thousand rounds of ammunition per month and built M18 Hellcat tank destroyer vehicles. Cadillac made

M5 Stuart tanks. Oldsmobile produced machine guns for airplanes. Pontiac built torpedoes. Ford plants assembled B-24 Liberators. Chevy made trucks (like troop transport trucks, not Silverados) and armored cars. Elsewhere in the world, Rolls-Royce produced the engine for the Spitfire fighters, while BMW made the engine for Germany's Focke-Wulf 190. Mitsubishi used Chinese and Korean slave labor to build the A6M Zero fighter plane, and Ferdinand Porsche designed and produced one version of the German Tiger tank. On a related note, Enzo Ferrari and Ferruccio Lamborghini were both race car enthusiasts who worked as mechanics for Italy, and after the war used their knowledge from those jobs to start their own supercar companies.

WASPS

The United States didn't use female pilots in combat roles, but the brave, experienced fliers of the Women Airforce Service Pilots (WASP) flew new, untested aircraft from factories in the United States straight to frontline bases in England and Europe. Over a thousand WASP pilots flew millions of miles in every type of plane assembled by the US. Thirty-eight lost their lives, either because of equipment failures or by being shot down by the enemy. WASP was commanded by Lieutenant Colonel Jackie Cochran, an air race "Speed Queen" who beat a hundred men to win the Bendix Cross Country Air Race in 1938. After the war, Cochran became an Air Force test pilot, was the first woman to travel faster than the speed of sound, and temporarily held the airspeed record by doing 1,429 miles an hour in an F-104 jet fighter.

GENERAL JIMMY STEWART

Bombing runs against Germany would last throughout the rest of the war, annihilating the German economy and ensuring air superiority for the Allies when they finally got around to attacking the Germans on D-Day (more on that in chapter 15). Gene Roddenberry, the inventor of *Star Trek*, flew eighty-nine missions in a B-17. James Stewart, a famous actor who received the Academy Award for best actor in 1940, flew more than twenty runs in the war, retired as a brigadier general, then came back to Hollywood and starred in *It's a Wonderful Life*, *Rear Window*, *Vertigo*, and a couple dozen other awesome movies. The highest-ranking officer killed in action while flying a B-17 was Brigadier General Nathan Bedford Forrest III, grandson of the famous Civil War Confederate general. He was shot down in 1943 while attacking U-boat bases on the French coast. During the war, nearly fifty thousand bomber aircraft would drop over two million tons of explosives on enemy cities and towns. It would take Germany decades to recover from the devastation.

KNOW YOUR VEHICLES

	Boeing B-17 Flying Fortress	Focke-Wulf 190 A-8
TYPE	Long-range strategic bomber	Interceptor aircraft
COUNTRY	United States	Germany
FIRST PRODUCED	1941	1944
LENGTH	74 feet, 4 inches	29 feet, 5 inches
WEIGHT	36,000 pounds (empty) 54,000 pounds (loaded)	10,800 pounds
ENGINE	Four 1,200-hp Wright R-1820-97 radial	BMW 801 D-2 radial
TOP SPEED	287 mph	408 mph
RATE OF CLIMB	900 feet per minute	2,350 feet per minute
CREW	10	1
ARMAMENT	Twelve .50-caliber machine guns Up to 17,600 pounds of bombs	Four 20mm cannons Two 13mm machine guns

The Focke-Wulf 190 was equipped with heavy weaponry to bring down the powerful B-17 bombers. It wasn't as good in an airplane-to-airplane dogfight as the Messerschmitt, but its extra weight gave it more stability when it was aiming at enemy planes. One-on-one, the 190s could pick a Flying Fortress apart. The only safety for the Allied bomber pilots was to stick together in tight formations so they could mass all their machine guns in one place.

14

THE WHITE MOUSE

Nancy Wake and the French Resistance

Various sectors of France
1940–1945

I don't see why we women should just wave our men a proud good-bye and then knit them balaclavas.

—Nancy Wake, Allied spy

NANCY WAKE WAS A PEERLESS WORLD WAR II special agent, saboteur, and resistance commander who survived four days of Gestapo interrogation and saved hundreds of downed Allied pilots from falling into the clutches of the Nazis. In the process, she blew up a couple of German supply depots, had a bounty of five million francs placed on her head, and once killed an SS storm trooper with her bare hands by apparently dishing out a judo chop to the throat.

Born to a dirt-poor family in New Zealand in 1912, Nancy Wake moved to Australia when she was two. Then her dad promptly abandoned Nancy, her mom, and her five brothers and sisters. Growing up in poverty, Wake left home at sixteen to work as a nurse in Sydney, Australia. At twenty, she moved to London to try to make a new life with about two hundred pounds sterling in her pocket. By twenty-two, this globe-trotting Aussie/Kiwi was living in Paris, working as a freelance newspaper journalist during the day and rocking out at the hottest Parisian nightclubs after dark. Wake could rarely be found without a double gin and tonic in her hand and designer cosmetics in her purse, and she had a reputation for drinking hard, telling dirty jokes, and then getting a tall, dark, and handsome Frenchman to pick up her tab.

In 1933 Wake's newspaper beat took her to Vienna to do a story on the new German chancellor, a guy named Adolf Hitler, so she headed out to see what the big deal was. Wake interviewed Hitler and then watched as gangs of Nazi thugs roamed the streets of Vienna beating up Jewish men and women. Wake, horrified by what she was seeing, vowed to oppose this Hitler fellow at any opportunity.

It wouldn't be long before she had her chance.

By the time the blitzkrieg made its way to the French countryside in 1940, Wake had been married to a millionaire

Nancy Wake, 1945

French industrialist for a few years. Her husband was called up to service, so Wake headed straight to the recruiting office and signed up to work as a nurse. She drove an ambulance during the invasion of Belgium, watched the Nazis steamroll everything before them in a cloud of dust, and then used her truck to help ferry British, Aussie, and New Zealander soldiers to evacuation points after it became painfully obvious that France was toast.

Nancy Wake, however, refused to evacuate with the rest

of the English and Commonwealth forces. She stayed behind in France, watched in horror as Hitler seized Paris, and then immediately used her husband's considerable wealth to shelter Royal Air Force pilots who had been shot down by Nazi antiaircraft defenses in France. Working out of a safe house she'd purchased outside Marseilles, Wake spent the first three years of the war getting fabricated identification cards, new clothes, and other cool James Bond spy stuff together for downed Allied pilots. She'd then ferry them across the Pyrenees mountains to Spain by sneaking them in trucks,

bribing guards with a bunch of cash, and doing whatever she could to get the pilots back to Britain safely. Her operation became such a major pain in Germany's operations that they put a five-million-franc reward on her head. Known only by her nickname, "the White Mouse," Wake at one point was on the top of the Gestapo's Most Wanted List. Which is a bad place to be.

If that wasn't scary enough, in 1943 the Germans started to figure out the White Mouse's true identity. In typical Gestapo way, they decided the best thing to do would be to capture Wake, put her up against a brick wall, and shoot her in the back of the skull. Luckily for Wake's skull, British spymasters and code breakers intercepted Gestapo communications ordering the arrest of the White Mouse and were able to relay the "RUN FOR IT" message to Wake before the Nazis knocked on her front door. She made a break for the Pyrenees mountains but was spotted by German SS officers while riding a train toward the border. Wake made her way through the car and jumped off the moving train like someone out of a James Bond movie. But as she was running for the cover of the woods, she was shot at and captured by the Germans and hauled off to the local Gestapo police station.

They tortured her for four days. She gave them nothing. Not even her real name.

Amazingly, she told the Gestapo so convincingly that she didn't know anything that they simply let her go free. A few

weeks later she was driving through the Pyrenees in the back of a coal truck, and from there it was just a quick boat ride through U-boat–infested waters until she was back in London.

Her husband wasn't so lucky. He was captured, tortured, and executed by the Nazis. This made Nancy Wake only angrier.

In London, the now-famous White Mouse was brought into the headquarters of the Special Operations Executive—Britain's awesome office of top secret spy stuff. Wake was trained in espionage, sabotage, and other useful skills, and then in April 1944 she jumped out of the back of a B-24 bomber in the middle of the night and parachuted into central France carrying a pistol, a radio, and a fat stack of French cash. Her chute got stuck in a tree on the way down, and when the local French Resistance leader said some obnoxious thing like "I wish all trees grew such beautiful fruit," she said (in perfect French), "Don't give me that French [nonsense]."

Now, the first group of Maquis (as in the French Resistance fighters, not the *Star Trek: Deep Space Nine* guys) she met chivalrously said, "Eh, forget this war thing, let's just kill this chick and take all her cash." But Wake escaped and fled across central France on foot in the middle of the night. She then linked up with a more gentlemanly Maquis Resistance cell and proceeded to impress every man there with her fearlessness in combat and her ability to drink them all under the

French Resistance (Maquis) fighters in La Tresorerie, France, 1944

table. In less than two months, she was a high-level officer responsible for acquiring and distributing weapons, ammunition, and communications equipment for an army of about seven thousand hardcore French Resistance fighters.

At the head of a group of dedicated, gun-toting Frenchmen, Nancy Wake spent most of 1944 leading wild guerrilla attacks on Nazi supply depots, rail stations, and communications facilities. In one raid, she killed a Nazi with her bare hands before he could raise an alarm. In another attack, she and some Maquis fighters rolled up to the local Gestapo headquarters in

Montluçon, France, shot the place up, lobbed some grenades, and killed thirty-eight members of the Reich's notorious secret police. When enemy spies were captured, Wake was the one who interrogated them and determined whether they would live or die. This was brutal work but necessary for the war effort. When supply drops were parachuted in behind enemy lines by Allied transport planes, Wake was the one who received the coordinates, made sure guys were there to pick up the gear, and distributed it to the men. Once, her cell engaged over ten thousand Germans from the Second SS Panzer Division to delay them as they were coming to the aid of the Germans being hit during D-Day. Wake's radio was destroyed when the truck she was driving was strafed by a Nazi dive-bomber—she responded by stealing a bicycle, riding it 125 miles in seventy-two hours to hook up with another Maquis cell, and immediately radioing London for assistance. On yet another occasion, Wake took command of a battle after her section leader died, then coordinated a strategic withdrawal that got her men out of a grim shoot-out with SS infantry without taking any further casualties.

When the war finally ended and it was time to hand out the medals, Nancy Wake found herself the most decorated Allied woman of World War II. She received the British George Medal, the American Medal of Freedom, the French Légion d'Honneur, and the French Croix de Guerre—that one three times. She was made a member of the Order of Australia. New Zealand named a street after her.

But Nancy Wake, the White Mouse of the French Resistance, hadn't done it for awards, medals, and recognition. She'd done it to liberate her homeland from the oppression of cruel, cold-blooded foreign invaders. Later in life, when asked why she sold a trio of Croix de Guerre medals, she said, "There's no point in keeping them....I'll probably go to hell and they'd melt there anyway."

She lived to be ninety-eight years old.

THE GESTAPO

One of the most feared names in Germany was that of the Gestapo—the Nazi secret police. Given free rein to do pretty much whatever they wanted to whomever they wanted, the Gestapo bypassed courts and regular cops and just straight-up kidnapped suspected Communists, Jews, Resistance agents, political enemies, and anyone else who didn't think Hitler was the best thing since snack packs. Using brutal methods, the Gestapo would torture and execute their enemies without giving them anything resembling a fair trial.

VIVE LA RÉSISTANCE

The French Resistance wasn't really some big, organized thing, and the *Maquis* is just a nickname for the groups of random dudes with guns who ran around the French forests shooting Nazis. Some, like the ones who tried to rob Nancy Wake, weren't the most trustworthy armed men on the planet, while others were highly efficient patriotic Frenchmen on a mission. There were a couple of larger Resistance groups as well, such as the one that organized a mass uprising in the Paris streets and threw out the Nazis as the Allies reached the outskirts of the city. Most groups recognized Charles de Gaulle as their leader, and pretty much all were funded through the British Special Operations Executive. The actual number of Resistance fighters will never be known, but during the war the Germans ordered the death, deportation, and torture of ninety thousand men and women suspected of being collaborators.

THE SOE

The Special Operations Executive (SOE) was created in July 1940 to undermine Hitler from within the countries he was occupying. Composed of around ten thousand agents—about a third of whom were women—the SOE provided spies and Resistance forces with forged papers, training, weapons, money, codes, communications equipment, and cool spy tech like a super-new invention called plastic explosives. The SOE sent agents to help Josip Tito's anti-Nazi guerrilla partisans in Yugoslavia, sabotaged railroad lines in Greece, armed half a million Frenchmen around the time of D-Day, and rescued Royal Air Force pilots in the Netherlands. The SOE's biggest accomplishment was probably an awesome undercover mission in February 1943, when six daring Norwegian SOE operatives parachuted into the waist-deep snow of Vemork, Norway, and blew up a lab where the Nazis were trying to create material for a nuclear bomb.

SPIES OF THE WESTERN FRONT

Agent Zigzag

A notorious womanizer, blackmailer, and safecracker in 1930s England, Eddie Chapman was a well-dressed bad guy with a flair for the dramatic. This dapper career crook fled England in 1939 after being arrested for blowing the safe of a fancy nightclub, only to find himself locked up in a Nazi-controlled French prison in 1940. Chapman picked the lock on his cell and escaped, but when he was recaptured, he agreed to work for the Nazis, parachuted into England, and then immediately offered his services to British intelligence. Known as "Agent Zigzag," Chapman spent the rest of the war pretending to be a German spy but actually working for the British. He was so good at his job that Hitler awarded him an Iron Cross medal for bravery, even though all the V-2 rocket target coordinates Chapman provided were totally wrong. He was never discovered, survived the war, and received complete forgiveness from the British government for all previous crimes.

Virginia Hall

An American woman who happened to be in Paris when the Nazis came rolling into town, Virginia Hall made her way to England and joined up with the SOE right when it was created in 1940. Sent to Paris under the guise of being a reporter for the *New York Post*, she helped train sabotage agents, forged fake IDs, mapped out parachute drop points for British commandos, set up a network of safe houses to protect spies from the Germans, and reported back to the British with information on enemy troop positions. Hall had a wooden leg (she had lost her limb in a hunting accident before the war), and her actions in undermining the Germans were so effective that the Gestapo had "the limping lady" high up on their Most Wanted list.

Count Robert Jean-Marie de la Rochefoucauld

This super-rich French count fled his homeland after the Nazis marked him as a "person of interest" in 1942, heading to England to offer his services to French general Charles de Gaulle. De Gaulle linked Rochefoucauld up with the SOE, who sent him back to France to help coordinate Resistance groups in the countryside. He blew up power stations and railroad lines but was eventually captured by the SS and sentenced to be executed as a spy. He escaped by jumping out of a moving truck, doubling back to the place where he got arrested, stealing a Gestapo limousine, and then leading the Germans on a high-speed chase through the city. He made his way back to England on a British submarine, then parachuted back into France just a month before D-Day. On his second tour of duty, he smuggled ninety pounds of explosives into a factory by hiding them inside hollowed-out loaves of bread and blew up the biggest Nazi ammunition factory in northern France. He was arrested again and escaped by faking a seizure, killing the guard, putting on the guy's uniform, and walking right out the front door. After escaping, he disguised himself as a nun and made his way to the nearest Resistance safe house.

Violette Szabo

Just nineteen years old when the war began, Violette Szabo was a young French woman with a newborn baby girl. Forced to flee to England after the Nazi attack, Szabo became enraged at the news that her husband, a brave officer in the French Foreign Legion, had been killed in battle with the Afrika Korps in October 1942. She enlisted with the SOE and was sent to Paris to spy on the enemy and, you know, occasionally blow things up in an awesome way. Never one to run away from a winnable firefight, Szabo battled squads of German soldiers and shot her way through several roadblocks, but she was eventually captured by the Gestapo in 1944 and executed at Ravensbrück concentration camp.

Agent Garbo

One of the most successful double agents in history, Juan Pujol Garcia almost single-handedly assured the success of the D-Day attack. An ordinary-looking, balding Spaniard who never fired a gun in anger, Garcia offered his services to the SOE but was turned down because they didn't think he had anything to offer. So he lied to the German intelligence agency, told them he was friends with a British diplomat, and offered to spy for them. They hired him, and Pujol spent the next couple of months creating an elaborate, insane network of totally fake spies who sent page after page of useless, incorrect information to the Nazis. Sitting in his apartment in Portugal with nothing more than a road map of London, a Frommer's guide to England, and a copy of the British railway schedule, Garcia convinced the entire Nazi intelligence service that he was manipulating a ring of twenty-seven (!) secret agents who had infiltrated key facilities across England.

At first the British intercepted these radio transmissions and freaked out, but when they realized all the info Garcia was sending was totally wrong they were like, "What the heck is going on here?" They tracked him down, relocated him to London, and put him to work convincing the Germans that the Allied invasion of France was going to land at Calais instead of Normandy. The Germans bought it, and even as landing craft were pulling up on Omaha Beach, Hitler held his troops back. He was convinced those landings were just a decoy, since his spymasters had told him that the attack was certainly coming at Calais.

KNOW YOUR VEHICLES

	BMW R75	Sd. Kfz. 251
TYPE	Motorcycle	Half-tracked armored personnel carrier
COUNTRY	Germany	Germany
FIRST PRODUCED	1941	1939
LENGTH	7 feet, 10 inches	19 feet
WEIGHT	930 pounds	8.6 tons
ARMOR	None	14 millimeters
ENGINE	26-hp 745cc flat-twin	99-hp Maybach HL 42 6-cylinder gasoline
TOP SPEED	59 mph	33 mph
CREW	1	2 plus 10 passengers
ARMAMENT	One 7.92mm machine gun in sidecar	One 7.92mm machine gun

Nancy Wake loved riding motorcycles, and the main Nazi bike was the BMW R75, a 745cc motorcycle that had a cool detachable sidecar that was usually equipped with a machine gun. It was fast, it excelled at tight turns, and it was generally very BMW-like. Nancy would generally have to look out for things like the Sd.Kfz. 251, an armored German troop transport that had two wheels in the front and a tank tread in the back. It was open-topped, and ten guys could easily pack in and each shoot over the side of it. There was also a heavy machine gun fixed in the front for extra pizzazz.

15

D-DAY

The Allied Invasion of Normandy

Omaha Beach, French Coast
June 6, 1944

This is it, men. Pick it up and put it on, you've got a one-way ticket and this is the end of the line. Twenty-Nine, let's go!

—Loudspeaker announcement to the Twenty-Ninth Infantry Division just before the Allied attack on Normandy

IT WAS A DARK, CLOUDY, FREEZING-COLD MORNING, just past dawn. Packed into a floating tin can with walls so high you had to stand on your toes to look over them, thirty men rocked through the misty ocean spray on five-foot waves that lifted their boat high in the air and dropped it hard, giving everyone that feeling you get on a roller coaster. Some men were praying. Some were hurling. Others were using their helmets to scoop out the ankle-deep seawater that had built up on the floor of the Landing Craft Assault (LCA).

A sharp whistling overhead was followed by a rumbling explosion off in the distance. Back out in the English Channel, Allied warships were chucking huge artillery shells at unseen targets on the coast ahead. Spitfires and B-17s streaked over, moving to targets farther inland.

The Coast Guardsman at the helm turned and screamed over the roar of the ocean: “Two minutes!”

More whistling. This time, however, it was followed by a huge explosion and a pillar of water blasting high into the

US troops approaching Omaha Beach, 1944

air. Officers yelled to keep heads down. Bullets fired from an unseen enemy pinged off the solid plate that was going to be the boat's landing ramp or splashed into the ocean beyond. Nearby, another LCA took a direct hit from an 88mm coastal artillery shell and was ripped apart in a ball of fire that sent men flying in every direction. Another craft struck an anti-ship mine hidden deep beneath the waves. The explosion blew off the bottom half of the boat, dumping its soldiers into the ocean. Most of them didn't resurface.

"Thirty seconds!" Men grabbed their rifles. The Coast Guardsman, steering by looking through a tiny slit in the steel plating of the ship, took a quick turn to avoid a mine that just barely peeked above the surface of the water.

With a jolt, the LCA touched ground. The metal landing ramp slammed down.

Almost immediately, a spray of machine-gun fire killed or wounded every man in the front of the ship. Those lucky enough to get through the screams, pinging, and thumps of bullets found themselves in waist-deep water, weighed down by sixty-pound backpacks. They needed to run fifty yards to the sandy beach and then another hundred yards across open ground in broad daylight to a seawall. Beyond that, along towering gray cliffs with perfect views of the beach, were two thousand German soldiers from the battle-hardened 352nd Infantry. They were hidden along the bluffs in bulletproof concrete bunkers outfitted with antitank cannons, mortars,

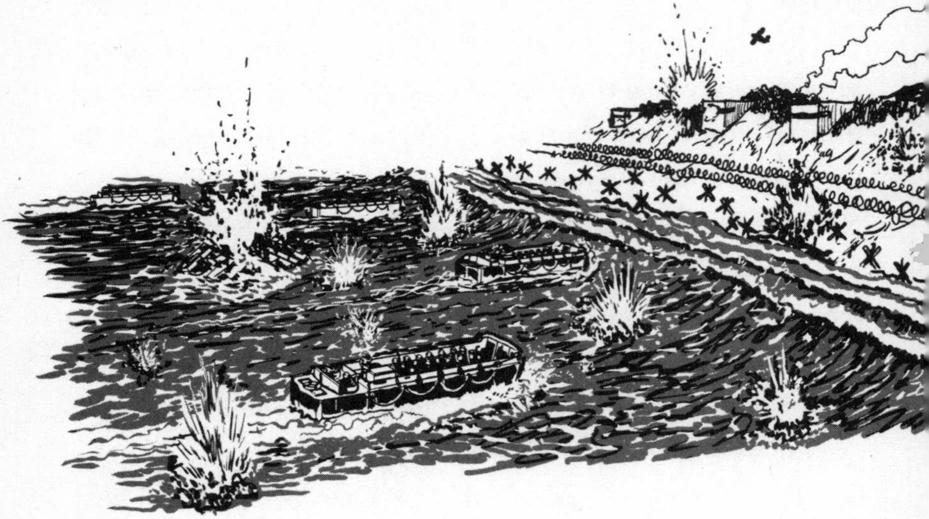

and at least eighty-five MG42 machine guns—rapid-firing weapons known as "Hitler's Buzz Saw."

It was six thirty AM on June 6, 1944. Just off the coast of the beach code-named "Omaha" on Allied planning maps, a hundred LCA vehicles were unloading three thousand men from the American First and Twenty-Ninth Infantry Divisions onto the shores of Nazi-occupied France.

D-Day had begun.

American losses in the first hour of D-Day on "Bloody Omaha" were horrific. German machine gunners, perfectly sighting in on the LCA craft, fired until their gun barrels were too hot to touch, spraying the entire beach with bullets from dozens of directions at once. Struggling with their gear and not exactly excited about the idea of running up a cliff toward eighty-five machine guns, the Americans still pressed forward, knowing they were just the tip of the overwhelming assault that was now beginning.

From his LCA just off the coast, Brigadier General Norman "Dutch" Cota watched with his fists clenched as the first wave of soldiers was hammered by a ferocious storm of gunfire. For the men of his Twenty-Ninth Infantry Division, mostly Virginia and Maryland National Guardsmen, this was

The first wave of troops landing on Omaha Beach, 1944

the first combat they had seen in the war. Some of them had lost their guns in the confusion, or their weapons became so jammed with sand and water that they wouldn't fire. Only about a third made it to the seawall. The rest were now scrambling for nonexistent cover or lying dead in the sand. The First Infantry, veteran warriors who had served in North Africa, were doing only slightly better.

Dutch's heart was with both units on Omaha that day. He had been the chief of staff for the First Infantry Division during their battles with Rommel's Afrika Korps, and in the summer of 1943 he had become the assistant commander of the Twenty-Ninth Infantry. He couldn't just sit there and watch his men get massacred. They needed leadership. They needed to get off that beach, storm the cliffs, move into the French towns beyond, and hook up with the men of the Eighty-Second, 101st, and British Sixth Airborne who had parachuted in the night before and were now fighting for their lives.

Dutch told his driver to take the LCA in, even though the mission plan didn't say anything about an assistant division commander hitting the beach with the second wave of infantry like some kind of suicidal lunatic.

The LCA driver, a Royal Navy guy, cranked the engine. Along the way, the LCA struck a mine, but for some reason it failed to explode and Dutch's boat kept flying. As it approached the coast, the ramp dropped hard into the ocean, and an immediate spray of German machine-gun fire killed a major and two staff officers.

Brigadier General Dutch Cota had a walking stick and an unlit cigar in his mouth, and his helmet's chin strap was unhooked (he was the only man in the Twenty-Ninth who was allowed to wear it this way). He calmly made his way past a burning hulk of a Sherman tank and started the 150 yards through knee-deep water toward the men at the seawall. To his left, an American colonel ran out of his boat firing a Bren machine gun from the hip, peppering the bluffs with bullets.

At the seawall, disorganized troops from the Twenty-Ninth, the First, and the Fifth Ranger Battalions hunkered behind the rocks, keeping their heads down as bullets whizzed past or ricocheted off the stone. Enemy artillery and mortar shells ranged closer with each shot, trying to blast them.

Then, out of nowhere, a fifty-year-old man with a walking stick in one hand and a Colt .45 automatic pistol in the other came hustling up. He said he was in charge now. Forget the mission plan, he told the men. We're not going up the path. We're climbing the bluff, and we're going to take these guys out. Then, famously, he told the Fifth Rangers, "Rangers, lead the way!"

This is the US Army Rangers' motto to this day.

Grabbing some cover, Cota directed a soldier with a Browning Automatic Rifle (also known as a BAR, a rapid-fire assault rifle) to open fire on an enemy machine-gun nest. You

don't have to kill them, or even aim, he said. Just put a lot of bullets close enough that they keep their heads down and stop shooting for a second. Then he ordered a guy to use a Bangalore mine (basically a bomb on the end of a stick) to blast through a thick hunk of barbed wire on the other side of the seawall. When he ordered his men to charge ahead, the first guy through the broken wire was ripped up by an enemy machine gun and died immediately. Everyone else lost their nerve.

Knowing what he had to do to make this mission work, Dutch Cota got up and ran through the broken wire, firing his pistol all the way. When the rest of the men saw their ultrabrave division commander racing ahead like a stone-cold warrior, they followed him immediately.

Dutch Cota was in pretty good shape, and he personally led the way for the men of the Twenty-Ninth. He took them a hundred yards through a minefield, broke into an enemy trench, wiped out the defenders, and then followed the trench to the base of the bluffs. From there, he, the Rangers, and the Twenty-Ninth Infantry made it up the bluffs, taking out bunkers and clearing enemy positions with hand grenades, M1 rifles, .45s, and rapid fire from BARs and tommy guns. Fighting every step of the way, Cota's makeshift command reached the top of the bluff, went a quarter mile off the coast, entered the town of Vierville, and linked up with troops from the 101st Airborne.

But Dutch Cota wasn't done. His men needed him.

So he went *back to Omaha Beach.*

With just a handful of men watching his back, Cota made his way to the beach—capturing five German soldiers in the process—and found another group of men from the third and fourth assault wave backed up against the seawall. Screaming, waving his pistol, and shouting orders, Cota ordered these guys to get up and moving. When he saw a perfectly operational bulldozer lying unmanned on the beach, he calmly asked, "Does anyone know how to drive this thing?" Some kid spoke up, and Cota just slapped him on the back and said, "That's the stuff!" The kid then spent the rest of the day bulldozing parts of the beach to make it easier for troops to get up the beach.

More men moved up and off the coastline. All along the English Channel, LCAs streamed ahead, bringing soldiers, trucks, supplies, and weapons. At one point, a British destroyer sailed straight up to the beach and fired point-blank into the bluff to continue clearing the Germans away. Army engineers braved incredible fire to clear out obstacles and make paths for more landing craft to reach safety. By nightfall, American forces would be a mile inland.

Omaha was just one of six beaches hit by the Allies during the D-Day invasion, but it was by far the bloodiest. A total of 4,413 men were dead, wounded, or missing in the attack, but the landing had succeeded. By the end of June, 850,000

Allied troops, 148,000 vehicles, and 570,000 tons of supplies had been brought from England and unloaded into France.

It was the beginning of the end for Hitler's power in Europe.

THE APPLE DOESN'T FALL FAR

The only other general to land in the early waves of soldiers on D-Day was Brigadier General Teddy Roosevelt Jr., son of the famous and awesomely over-the-top American president. Even though this fifty-seven-year-old officer had arthritis and a heart condition and had to walk with a cane, he specifically asked to be in the first wave of soldiers at Utah Beach, going ashore with his Fourth Infantry Division. Utah wasn't as bad as Omaha, but as mortars rained explosives down on the landing zones, people noted that TR Jr. "acted more annoyed than afraid." The Fourth suffered fewer than two hundred casualties, but he bravely stood up on the beach directing troops, giving orders, and helping bring men ashore. Thanks to him, the Fourth had unloaded twenty thousand men and eighteen hundred vehicles by nightfall and had already linked with members of the 101st Airborne in the city beyond.

I LIKE IKE

Coordinating the armies of America, the United Kingdom, Poland, France, and a couple of other countries as they prepared to undertake the largest land-sea operation in human history isn't exactly the same thing as ordering a Happy Meal at McDonald's. So to keep everything under control, the Allies appointed American general Dwight D. "Ike" Eisenhower to be Supreme Allied Commander. A mild-mannered Texan (yes, there is such a thing) who had basically built the Army Tank Corps from scratch, Ike had one main gift: He could get a lot of fiery, wildly different personalities to work together. He kept guys like Patton (more about him in chapter 18) and Montgomery from killing each other, coordinated air drops and supply lines, and did an excellent job of running the entire Allied war in the West smoothly. After World War II, he would command NATO in Europe, then be elected to the first of two terms as president of the United States in 1953. As president, Ike negotiated the end of the Korean War, ended racial segregation in the military, signed two civil rights acts into law, and created the idea of constructing interstate highways.

OPERATION VALKYRIE

After the Normandy campaign, Erwin Rommel told Hitler that the war was over. Echoing other German officers, Rommel said that rather than sacrifice German lives, it was time to make peace with the United States and Britain and to direct the Germans' efforts against the Russians instead. Hitler angrily refused. A month later, on July 20, 1944, a group of German Army officers led by an eye-patch-wearing colonel named Claus von Stauffenberg rigged up a briefcase bomb and put it under a desk in Hitler's war strategy room. The bomb demolished the room, blowing Hitler's pants off and killing three of his men, but the Führer lived. And he wasn't really happy about almost being disintegrated by plastic explosives. He ordered the arrest and execution of nearly five thousand people in connection with the plot. To this day, we don't know whether Rommel was in on it, but nevertheless the Gestapo gave the popular commander two options: Kill yourself, or we will arrest you and kill your family. He committed suicide on October 14, 1944, and was buried with full military honors.

THAT'S A LOT OF PEOPLE

The standard operational infantry unit in the United States military during World War II was the division, which consisted of roughly 14,250 men arranged into three regiments. The army fielded ninety divisions in the war, sixty-eight in Europe and twenty-two in the Pacific. As of January 1944, there were 4.5 million men in the US Army, a number that included the 1.8 million members of the United States Army Air Force (the air force hadn't broken off and become its own service branch yet). The Marine Corps had another six divisions of their own, totaling about 405,000 men. The navy fielded an additional 2 million troops, including 172,000 members of the US Coast Guard.

CANADIANS IN THE WAR

Anyone who thinks Canadians are all a bunch of easygoing, laid-back, superpolite pushovers just needs to watch a professional hockey game or a documentary on lumberjacking to realize that these are some of the roughest people in North America. Canadian forces were there on the front lines at D-Day, storming the coast at Juno Beach despite heavy enemy opposition, and they provided some of the most intensely hard-fighting soldiers in the entire Allied forces. It's for good reason that Winston Churchill once said, "If I had English officers, Canadian soldiers, and American technology, I could conquer the world."

Here are just a few of their stories.

Smokey Smith

Ernest "Smokey" Smith was such a bad kid in school that when World War II broke out, he drove to another city to enlist in the army because he didn't want to be stationed in the same military unit as his teachers. He was promoted from private to corporal nine times during the war, but all nine times he was dropped back down to private because he never listened to orders and had a bad habit of only showing up for duty when there was a battle to fight. He was still a good guy to have on your side, though. In one battle, his unit was attacked by German tanks and infantry, so Smokey grabbed a bazooka and a tommy gun and went on a one-man rampage, shredding Nazi tanks at point-blank range. In another epic battle, Smith destroyed three German Panther tanks, a half-track, a self-propelled artillery piece, and a scout car; took out nearly thirty German soldiers; and heroically pulled a wounded friend out of the middle of the battle-field.

Leo Major

This one-eyed French Canadian sniper performed tons of awesomely heroic deeds of ridiculousness during the Second World War. But none of them come close to the time he liberated the Dutch town of Zwolle all by himself. Major wore a cool Nick Fury–style pirate eye patch because he'd taken a Nazi grenade to the face during the Normandy campaign, and in April 1945 he and another guy volunteered to scout ahead of the main Canadian forces and see what was going on in Zwolle. Well, as he was peering through his scope to see what was up, a German machine gun spotted him, opened fire, and killed Major's best friend. Leo slung three machine guns over his back, grabbed a sack of hand grenades, and ran screaming into town, hurling bombs everywhere. He kicked open the door of the SS officers' dining room and riddled it with bullets. He burned down the headquarters of the Gestapo. The Nazis, thinking they were under attack by an entire army, bolted, leaving the town solely in the hands of Leo Major.

Tommy Prince

A member of the Brokenhead band of the Ojibwe Indian tribe in rural Manitoba, Canada, Tommy Prince was the toughest and most feared man in the "Devil's Brigade," an elite unit of American and Canadian soldiers. An expert in wilderness survival and tracking, Prince could allegedly travel through the thickest forest at a dead run without making a sound and was such a killer marksman he could put six bullets through an ace of spades from a hundred feet away. Undertaking commando operations in Italy and Germany, Prince made a specialty of sneaking into German bases in the middle of the night and silently killing everyone in their sleep. Well, usually he'd kill them. Sometimes he'd just steal their boots off their feet or tie their shoelaces together as a way of scaring the crap out of them.

James Doohan

If you've ever watched the original *Star Trek* TV show, you'd probably be pretty surprised to find out that the guy who played Scotty isn't actually Scottish. He's Canadian, and that accent he has on the show is totally fake. James Doohan left his abusive family as a teenager and enlisted in the Royal Canadian Artillery, deploying at Juno Beach during the Normandy landings. Rushing ahead into a hail of gunfire, Doohan killed two snipers and was wounded six times in the chest, hand, and leg. As soon as he recovered he transferred to the Air Force and became a pilot, where he was infamous for flying his Hurricane at altitudes so low that he could maneuver it underneath the wires on a telephone pole.

KNOW YOUR VEHICLES

	U-110	HMS *Bulldog*
TYPE	Attack submarine, Type 9B U-boat	B-class destroyer
COUNTRY	Germany	United Kingdom
COMMISSIONED	1940	1931
LENGTH	251 feet	323 feet
DISPLACEMENT	1,158 tons	1,523 tons
MAX DEPTH	985 feet	N/A
ENGIN	Two MAN 9-cylinder diesels	Two Parsons geared steam engines
TOP SPEED	17 knots surface, 7.6 under-water	35 knots (40 mph)
CREW	56	142
ARMAMENT	Four 533mm bow torpedo tubes Two 533mm stern torpedo tubes One 105mm deck cannon One 20mm antiaircraft cannon	Four 4.7-inch cannons Two 40mm antiaircraft guns Eight 533mm torpedo tubes Two depth charge projectors

Most American soldiers got to Britain by boat rather than by air, and soldier transports were under the constant threat of attack from the Nazi U-boats, which were ravaging the shipping lanes in the North Atlantic. German subs relied on the element of surprise, trying to sneak in, sink their enemies' transports, then slide silently away before sub-hunting destroyer ships could arrive. Allies used aircraft and sonar to detect U-boats, and if they found one, they could drop a depth charge (an underwater bomb that explodes when it hits a certain depth). In 1941 the HMS *Bulldog* hit U-110 with a depth charge, causing a leak in the U-boat's hull that forced it to come to the surface and surrender. The British troops captured an Enigma code machine on the sub, which allowed them to crack the German military code.

16

GURKHA ASSAULT

The Battle for Mortar Bluff

Bishenpur, India
June 26, 1944

Better to die than live a coward.

—Motto of the Royal Gurkha Rifles

IF YOU WERE GOING TO MAKE A LIST OF THE MOST face-crushingly hardcore military organizations that ever existed, you would have to carve out a spot in the top three for the ferocious Gurkha soldiers of the British Army.

Recruited from the dirt-poor, dangerous foothills of Nepal's Himalaya Mountains, the Gurkhas are a lights-out group of warriors who have served in the British Army with honor and distinction for over two hundred years. In their dedicated service to the Queen, these short, humorless, ultradangerous killers helped the Crown put down rebellions in India in the nineteenth century, fearlessly assaulted German machine guns in both world wars, and continue to terrify Taliban fighters in the mountains of Afghanistan to this day. Cold, calculating, incredibly brave, and completely brutal in hand-to-hand combat, these guys are famous not only for being some of the most savage warriors on the planet, but also for carrying a deadly eighteen-inch curved knife known as a *kukri* with them at all times. The *kukri* is a weird-looking weapon because the blade is on the inside of the curve (as opposed to the outside like a samurai sword or a cavalry saber). It's said that Gurkhas are trained in a method of attack with this thing that is almost completely unblockable by the enemy.

And they love any opportunity to use their *kukris* in combat.

In the early months of 1944, the Imperial Japanese Army continued its rampaging expansion across Asia, launching a

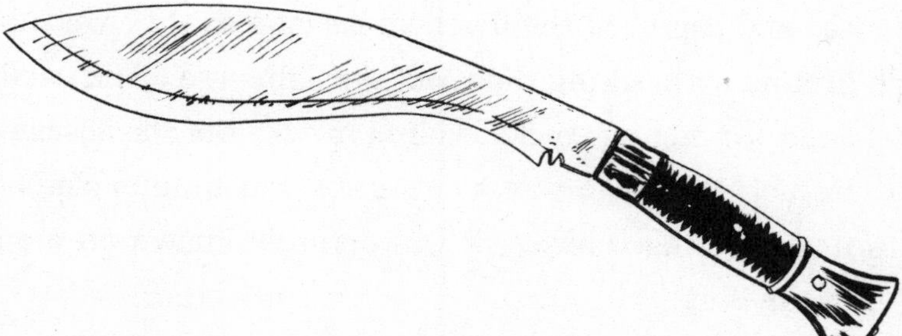

full-on attack into the British-controlled regions of Burma and Thailand. Hoping to destroy the Allied garrison at Imphal in India, the Japanese went after these regions because they wanted to cut off supply routes to the Chinese guerrillas and possibly even open the way for a full-on assault on India itself. They somehow moved a mind-boggling force of ninety thousand battle-hardened veterans through the trackless Indiana Jones monkey jungle of Southeast Asia, came screaming out of nowhere, and attacked British bases at Imphal and Kohima to do this. The brave men of the Seventeenth "Black Cat" Indian Infantry Division were cut off in Imphal without resupply, but they fought hard, receiving airdrops of everything from bullets to paratroopers to keep struggling against the unrelenting attack.

The battle reached a turning point in June 1944 when the Japanese seized a critical position overlooking the only road leading from Imphal to the main British resupply depot at Bishenpur. The Allies fought bitterly, but on the night of June 24, a relentless assault by Japanese troops overran the British defenses and captured the position. As long as they held the high ground overlooking the road, the Japanese could easily drop a mortar on any trucks leading in or out of the besieged city. In fact, the ridge was so good for chucking explosives onto unsuspecting vehicles, it was actually known on maps as "Mortar Bluff."

It was absolutely vital that the Allies retake this position as quickly as possible so they could bring more men and supplies to the front lines at Imphal.

Naturally, they called in the Gurkhas to get the job done.

This wouldn't be the first time that Agansing Rai of the Second Battalion, Fifth Royal Gurkha Rifles, went head-to-head with frontline Japanese troops. He had been part of the unit in 1941 and saw much of his unit wiped out while facing impossible odds during the Japanese invasion of Burma back in 1942. Now he was eager for revenge.

It wasn't going to be easy. Mortar Bluff was at the top of a supersteep hill with absolutely no cover between the Gurkhas

Gurkhas assaulting an enemy position, Tunisia, 1943

and the enemy machine guns and artillery. Worse yet, the bluff backed up against a thick jungle, where the Japanese had dug trenches and built bunkers to defend their post, and there was no telling how many guys they had lined up and ready to fight.

But when Agansing Rai received orders to take his men in on an attack, he didn't even flinch.

On the morning of June 26, the men of Second Battalion, Fifth Royal Gurkha Rifles, came charging out of the dense jungle and began racing up the steep cliff toward Mortar Bluff. Japanese machine guns thumped rounds down at them, shredding up the jungle and the hillside with murderous fire. They also brought out a 37mm cannon, a big, scary-looking artillery piece designed specifically to blast enemy infantry to smithereens, and laid into the headstrong Gurkhas with everything they had.

Running hard behind their twenty-four-year-old naik (basically a corporal), the men of Rai's section forced their way eighty yards uphill through intense machine-gun and cannon fire and then finally dove for cover behind a rocky ridge near the top of the cliff. Realizing that many of his men were wounded or dead, and that those who had lived were going to get chopped to pieces if they hung around too long, Agansing Rai reloaded his Thompson submachine gun, grabbed a grenade, hopped up, and made a break for the closest Japanese trench. He charged ahead, firing and throwing

his grenade, then leapt into the trench and pulled out his Gurkha knife.

Agansing Rai killed three enemy troops in hand-to-hand combat, cutting and swinging like a madman with his blade. His men, inspired by this display of ferocity, ran ahead, diving into other trenches along Mortar Bluff and wiping out machine-gun and artillery crews. When Rai was done clearing his own position, he continued to another machine-gun nest and took out three more enemy soldiers.

But this was just the beginning. When the Japanese in the jungle saw Mortar Bluff overrun by Gurkhas, they all turned their machine guns and opened fire on it. This only served to make Agansing Rai even angrier. After grabbing a couple of *live grenades* and throwing them back at the Japanese, he ordered the last two surviving men in his squad to cover him. Then this blood-raging Gurkha went on a one-man assault against a Japanese bunker, running across another open field into the jungle. Firing his tommy gun with one hand and lobbing grenades with the other, Rai sprinted to the jungle, jumped into the trench, pulled his knife, and took out four enemy troops with it, deflecting their rifle swings and laying into them with his blade. The surviving Japanese wisely ran for it. Then Naik Agansing Rai calmly made his way back to Mortar Bluff to regroup with the rest of his unit.

It had been bloody, costly, and ultraviolent, but the men of Company C, Second Battalion, Fifth Royal Gurkha Rifles, had captured Mortar Bluff and reopened the only supply and communications road from the main segment of British India to the besieged, beleaguered, outnumbered Allied forces desperately fighting in Imphal.

Now they had to hold it.

Rai's platoon leader was Subedar Netrabahadur Thapa, another tough Gurkha warrior, and he immediately told the forty-one surviving men on Mortar Bluff that they weren't out of this just yet. The Japanese had been pushed back, sure, but they were a vicious enemy, and they weren't going to pack up and walk home just because a couple of Nepalese guys had stuck knives in their eyes. Thapa had his men reposition machine guns, fortify the trenches, and prepare for a Japanese counterattack.

It came a few hours later, just around sunset.

The Japanese assault began with an artillery bombardment from 37mm and larger 75mm cannons that rained explosive shells down on the Gurkhas. Then, while their ears were still ringing from the explosions, the Gurkhas saw a full company of over two hundred Japanese infantry charging out of the dark jungle toward them. The Gurkhas fought hard with machine guns and rifle fire, laying into the Japanese, but every time the Japanese were pushed back, they simply regrouped and attacked again.

It was pitch-dark and raining in sheets as wave after wave of determined, heavily armed Japanese infantry poured into the trenches like a tsunami of bayoneted pointiness. The

Gurkhas, exhausted from fighting all day long, battled with whatever they had, striking out with knives and rifles in an unremitting battle against an almost endless swarm of troops. By four AM, over half of Thapa's brave defenders had been wounded, knocked out, or killed, but the rest fought on. With a rallying pump-up speech, Thapa regrouped his Gurkhas, assembled them at the command post, and launched a desperate bayonet attack to nail the swarming Japanese infantry. The brave commander was taken out by a grenade while leading his men, but the Gurkhas slammed into the Japanese *kukris*-first, hammering them with rifles and machine guns at point-blank range.

By first light, Agansing Rai was one of the few men left standing atop Mortar Bluff. He was surrounded by the bodies of his allies and his enemies alike. But the Gurkhas had held.

The Second Battalion, Fifth Royal Gurkha Rifles, lost close to eight hundred men in the fighting around Imphal, but thanks in no small part to their heroism, the garrison at Imphal was able to hold off the enemy attack and shatter the Japanese assault force. The Japanese were forced back toward China and would never again have the manpower to mount an offensive against the Allies in Asia. Their empire was now beginning to crumble around them on both land and sea.

HAPPILY EVER AFTER

For their heroism in the battle, both Agansing Rai and Netrabahadur Thapa received the Victoria Cross, the highest award bestowed by Great Britain for valor in combat. At the ceremony in January 1945, Rai was asked by a reporter what he was thinking when he led his attack. His response? "I forget." He survived the war, got married, had five kids, and lived to be eighty years old.

COME AND FIGHT A GURKHA

Another amazing Gurkha warrior was Lachhiman Gurung of the Eighth Royal Gurkha Rifles, who received a Victoria Cross for single-handedly holding his position against a huge wave of Japanese attackers. His squad was killed in a Japanese charge, and then the enemy started lobbing grenades into Gurung's foxhole. He kept throwing them back, until one of them exploded in his hand, blowing off a bunch of fingers and spraying his face with shrapnel. This, naturally, just made him mad. Gurung pulled his *kukri*, drew a line in the sand, and shouted, "Come and fight a Gurkha!" For the next four hours he loaded and fired his bolt-action rifle with one hand, holding off two hundred Japanese with just his gun and grenades. When the sun rose the next morning, there were thirty-one dead enemy soldiers around him.

KNOW YOUR VEHICLES

	Type 97 Chi-Ha	M3 Lee
TYPE	Medium tank	Medium tank
COUNTRY	Japan	United States (purchased by Great Britain)
FIRST PRODUCED	1936	1941
LENGTH	18 feet, 1 inch	18 feet, 6 inches
WEIGHT	16.5 tons	30 tons
ARMOR	28 millimeters	50 millimeters
ENGINE	170-hp Mitsubishi V-12 diesel	400-hp Continental R975 EC2
TOP SPEED	24 mph	26 mph
CREW	4	6
ARMAMENT	One 57mm Type 57 cannon Two 7.7mm machine guns	One 75mm M2/M3 cannon One 37mm M5/M6 cannon Three .30-06 caliber machine guns

The Japanese attack was spearheaded by sixty-six tanks from the Fourteenth Tank Regiment, an elite armored unit that had crushed Allied positions during the 1942 conquest of British Burma. By Imphal, however, the Japanese tanks were massively outmatched by the M3 Lee, an American-built tank that was really crazy-looking. It had a huge forward-facing cannon in the hull and a smaller rotating turret coming out the top. Crewed by Scots, Brits, Canadians, and Indians, the M3 "General Lee" led the way for the infantry assaults that broke the Japanese lines.

17

LAST STAND AT LEYTE

USS Johnston *at the Battle off Samar*

Straits of Samar, Philippines
October 25, 1944

This will be a fight against overwhelming odds from which survival cannot be expected. We will do what damage we can.

—Lieutenant Commander Robert W. Copeland, commanding officer, USS *Samuel B. Roberts*

THE IMPERIAL JAPANESE NAVY WARSHIP *Yamato* was an 862-foot-long wall of gun-toting steel. It was so impossibly humongous that if you could somehow plant it stern-first into the ground it would stand 200 feet taller than the Seattle Space Needle! This mega-warship weighed in at 72,800 tons fully loaded (one ton is about the same weight as a large dairy cow), thanks in part to the fact that it was completely covered in armor plating a foot and a half thick on all sides. The *Yamato*'s top deck was jam-packed with a brain-melting array of weaponry so over-the-top intense it makes the Death Star look like the Cinderella Castle at Disney World, including thirty-three cannons of different sizes and 160 antiaircraft machine guns and autocannons. The *Yamato* also had three huge rotating turrets, each of which was equipped with three jumbo eighteen-inch-wide mega-cannons—weapons that, to this day, are the largest guns ever mounted on a warship. It was home to twenty-five hundred sailors for months at a time, the biggest battleship in human history, a tremendous feat of modern engineering, and the flagship of the Imperial Japanese Navy. If you saw this thing represented as a boss in a video game, you'd shake your head and be like, "Yeah right, nobody could build something like that in *real* life."

And now, at the head of twenty-two other heavy cruisers and battleships, the superbattleships *Yamato* and *Musashi* (more on this ship at the end of the chapter) were steaming straight-on into combat against the weakest part of the US Navy. And the Americans had no idea they were coming.

It was October 1944, and the war was slowly turning against the Japanese. Despite epic last stands and heroic resistance by some of the world's most stout-hearted fighting men, the Japanese were systematically forced off their island bases across the Pacific by repeated assaults from US Marines at places like Guadalcanal, Peleliu Island, Tarawa, and Saipan. Now the Americans were rolling up on retaking the Philippines, which had fallen to the Japanese way back at the beginning of the war and was an absolutely vital source of gasoline and oil. As American landing craft under General Douglas MacArthur began streaming Army and Marine infantry onto the island, the Japanese knew they had to lay it all on the line to crush the attack.

The landings were protected by the ships of the US Navy, but the Philippines is a weird place. It's made up of a bunch of small islands, and there are plenty of straits and waterways where a big ship can sneak around without being noticed. Japanese admiral Soemu Toyoda planned to use this to full advantage with a crazy aquatic blitzkrieg-style pincer move to psych out the Americans. First, one group would lure the American aircraft carrier fleet out of the area with a fake attack by four Japanese carriers that were so underequipped they didn't even have planes on them. Then Toyoda's ships would launch a two-pronged attack through the straits of the Philippines. One group of battleships would attack from the south to engage the Americans there, while the *Yamato* would head straight up the undefended middle and start dropping bullets the size of Ferraris onto American troop transports and soldiers on the beach.

The plan worked, even though it was a little more painful than Toyoda had hoped. Japanese aircraft carriers drew the American carriers away from the Philippines, but most were sunk or damaged in the process. In the south, the Japanese fleet entered the Surigao Strait, where there were a couple of American battleships eager to say hello to them: the USS *West Virginia*, *Maryland*, *Tennessee*, *California*, and *Pennsylvania*. All five of those mighty warships had been repaired, rebuilt, and/or upgraded since they were torched by the Japanese at Pearl Harbor, and they got a little stone-cold revenge by plastering the attacking enemy fleet so hard it sank most of their ships and killed their commanding officer.

But then the Japanese sprang their trap.

At seven thirty AM on October 25, 1944, a lone recon pilot from Admiral Clifton Sprague's Task Unit 77.4.3 frantically radioed in an enemy contact to his commanding officer: The largest battleship on earth had been spotted, along with twenty-two supporting battleships, destroyers, and heavy cruisers. Bearing three-four-zero, range twenty miles, closing fast at thirty knots.

Sprague's command was a small submarine-hunting light task force nicknamed "Taffy-3." It consisted of three destroyers, four smaller escort ships, and six light aircraft carriers known as escort carriers. These were basically merchant ships that had been outfitted with a small flight deck that held only about thirty planes. And now the small task force was suddenly the only thing standing between tens of thousands of unprotected American soldiers and the largest battleship squadron in human history.

To give you some idea of what we're looking at here, just one of the *Yamato*'s eighteen-inch gun turrets (and it had three of them) weighed more than the largest warship under Sprague's command.

Sprague had basically zero time to react, and moments after he'd had his mind blown by that insane radio message, a shrieking barrage of eighteen-inch shells whistled past his flagship, throwing up a huge fountain of seawater hundreds of feet in the air. He ordered his carriers to accelerate to attack speed, turn hard, get their planes in the air, and then break and run for it (they were too vulnerable and important to stick around).

The Japanese Center Force closed in. Admiral Takeo Kurita, aboard his superbattleship *Yamato*, ordered his ships to run down the Americans and annihilate them. Cannons opened fire all across his fleet—the eighteen-inchers from the *Yamato*, twelve-inch guns from four regular-sized battleships,

The USS *Johnston*

and a substantial variety of deadly guns from six heavy cruisers, two light cruisers, and eleven destroyers, each of which was the same size as the three American destroyers.

Then, out of nowhere, one of the American destroyers turned hard, pointed the front of the ship straight at the *Yamato*, and rocketed forward at maximum speed.

DD-557, the USS *Johnston,* was commanded by Lieutenant Commander Ernest E. Evans, a Cherokee/Creek Indian from Oklahoma. He had already received a Bronze Star for a valiant battle against enemy submarines and had sworn never to back down or show fear. Now this warrior was leading his small ship on a one-man suicide charge against the entire Japanese Center Force, with nothing less than the survival of thousands of American soldiers and Marines hanging in the balance.

Evans ordered his men to deploy a smoke screen by adding extra oil to the boiler room engines. This caused a horrible-looking, non-eco-friendly cloud of thick black smoke to come piping out of the *Johnston*'s smokestacks, obscuring the Japanese commanders' vision and making it harder for them to aim their cannons at the rest of Taffy-3. Knowing that he needed to get in close with the enemy to fire his torpedoes (the only weapons he had that could do anything to a battleship or heavy cruiser), Evans ordered his helmsman to go to full flank speed but to zigzag back and forth in the water to dodge enemy gunfire. All around him, water started

Destroyers laying a smoke screen
(the white splashes are impacts from enemy shells)

shooting up as two dozen enemy warships began laying a curtain of fire in his direction.

A *Fletcher*-class destroyer like the USS *Johnston* was 376 feet long, weighed 2,700 tons, and had a crew of 273 men. It was equipped with ten torpedo tubes, five Mark 12 five-inch guns, and seventeen antiaircraft guns, and could do a top speed of thirty-five knots, which is like forty miles an hour. It was now racing across open water in broad daylight toward Japanese fleet ships that could launch a bullet the size of a refrigerator a distance of fifteen miles.

Still, despite some of the most one-sided odds of any battle ever, the *Johnston* zigzagged ahead, hurling herself through towers of seawater as hundreds of shells and cannon shots whizzed past. Overhead, American Avenger and Hellcat attack aircraft whooshed by, making attack runs even though they hadn't had time to equip with torpedoes or bombs and were firing machine guns at armored steel warships.

Somehow miraculously closing to five miles, Evans's ship opened fire with its five-inch guns. Cranking off over two hundred rounds in less than five minutes, the crew of the *Johnston* fought heroically, loading and firing until their cannons glowed. Bullets smashed into the Japanese cruisers, which returned fire at this one determined attacker, though somewhat unbelievably, the *Johnston* still avoided taking any hits.

After zigzagging at top speed across twenty miles of open water with no cover other than a black cloud of smoke and ineffective machine-gun fire from planes, the USS *Johnston* zeroed in on the heavy cruiser *Kumano*, a frontline warship over twice its size, and unleashed a storm of ship-incinerating torpedoes at point-blank range.

Ernest Evans's men scored a direct hit. A huge explosion rocked the *Kumano*, cracking it in half and smacking off the front part of the ship.

Then the Japanese ships found their range.

A sixteen-inch shell from the battleship *Kongo* ripped through the *Johnston*'s boiler, killing its engine, while a second shell from a different ship hit the AA gun ammo storage room, setting off a huge explosion. A third hit rocked Evans's bridge, smashing the communications and radar systems and spraying Evans with white-hot shrapnel. He was badly burned and lost two fingers, and his face was covered with wounds, but even though half his shirt was blown off, he ran out onto the deck and ordered his men to keep fighting.

Then he saw something incredible.

It was the rest of Taffy-3: two destroyers and four destroyer escorts, all racing ahead, trailing black smoke, coming to support the *Johnston* in its one-ship attack.

Evans stood at the railing saluting as the American ships churned past him and opened fire.

An epic battle raged for the next hour, as seven heroic little American warships traded face punches with the largest surface fleet in naval warfare history. First, the destroyer USS *Heermann* launched torpedoes at the *Yamato*, forcing it to take evasive actions. It wasn't hit, but the slow-turning radius of the gigantic ship accidentally ended up taking it way out of the center of the fighting. Seeing that he was losing control, Admiral Kurita ordered a "general attack," meaning every Japanese commander was on his own, and the fighting turned into a furious ship-to-ship melee. Armor-piercing bombs from an Avenger aircraft damaged the cruiser *Suzuya*, forcing it to withdraw. The battleship *Haruna* was rocked by a direct torpedo hit. The tiny, undergunned, unarmored destroyer escort *Samuel B. Roberts* closed in so tight to the heavy cruiser *Chokai* that the *Chokai* couldn't lower its guns enough to hit the *Roberts*. The *Chokai* was rocked by six hundred rounds of five-inch fire at point-black range and immobilized.

In the thick of the fighting, the crew of the *Johnston* noticed that a detachment of five enemy destroyers had separated from the battle and were making a torpedo run on the escort carriers. With no electrical power, no communications, no torpedoes, and a broken engine that was only operational because it was being hand-cranked by two dudes standing in a room being flooded by ocean water, the *Johnston* took a sharp turn and raced to face off against five ships that were all its equal in size. Evans hurtled toward the lead destroyer,

coming in out of nowhere and throwing it off course so all its torpedoes went well wide of the American carriers. Then he parked his ship in the middle of all five of them and started firing like crazy in every direction.

The battle raged on for another hour. The *Johnston* dished out huge hits but was pounded hard at close range. Back in the thick of the fighting, the destroyers *Hoel* and *Heermann* took hits from enemy ships, crippling them and sinking the *Hoel*, which continued to fire its five-inch guns even as it was slipping below the waves. The *Roberts* was drilled with shells and its crew abandoned ship, and the other destroyer escorts were all damaged as well.

Finally, with all its guns knocked out, its engines flooded, and the entire ship on fire, Ernest Evans ordered the crew of the *Johnston* to abandon ship. The brave, seriously wounded navy officer was last seen running up and down the decks, helping his men get out alive.

Out of torpedoes, the five Japanese destroyers headed off to rejoin their main force. But the crews saluted the American sailors who were now floating in life jackets in the water. Even though they'd spent all morning fighting each other, the Japanese sailors had to respect the bravery of Evans and his crew.

The Battle off Samar Island lasted two and a half hours. The United States lost two destroyers, an escort carrier, and a destroyer escort, and every other ship in Taffy-3 was

US Navy sailors pulled from the water after the battle

damaged to some degree. A total of 792 crew were dead, 768 were wounded, and many survivors were forced to float around in shark-infested waters for over two days before finally being rescued. In their heroic struggle, they'd destroyed two enemy heavy cruisers, damaged two others, and wrecked a battleship.

More important, they'd single-handedly stopped the Japanese Center Force from thwarting the invasion of the Philippines. After having so many ships damaged in the fight and realizing that American reinforcements wouldn't be far behind, battle group *Yamato* turned around and sailed out of the Philippines.

MATCHING SET

The superbattleship *Yamato* was one of a pair, if you can believe that. The other one, the *Musashi*, was also present off the coast of the Philippines, but it was destroyed super-early on in the fighting when aircraft from the USS *Intrepid* were like, "What the heck is that thing," and attacked it with everything they had. It took more than twenty direct bomb and torpedo hits to bring it down.

NAMESAKES

The USS *Johnston* was named for John V. Johnston, a US Navy officer from the American Civil War. Commanding a gunboat on the Mississippi, Johnston had participated in the shelling of Vicksburg, and then later had fought off a group of Confederate raiders who were threatening a Union supply base in Louisiana. As for the IJN *Yamato*, this Japanese warship was named after the clan that had founded the Japanese civilization in the fourth century and gave rise to the emperors.

RAID ON CABANATUAN

The Japanese were part of a warrior culture that, without fail, either fought to the death or committed suicide. They didn't even know how to think about surrendering, and the Japanese looked at prisoners of war as men who had no honor and deserved no respect. So when the Philippines fell in 1942 and the Japanese took seventy-five thousand prisoners of war, they kept the prisoners in miserable conditions, worked them to death, and sent them on long forced marches—the 1942 Bataan Death March killed eleven thousand Americans over the course of five days. One of the most savage prison camps was the one at Cabanatuan in the Philippines, where men were given little food and no medicine. Fearful that the Japanese would execute five hundred prisoners at Cabanatuan after the US landings, America ordered a commando raid to go in and get those men out alive. To assist, they called on the services of Captain Juan Pajota, a hardcore Filipino guerrilla who had been leading an underground resistance movement against the Japanese for the last two years. While the US Army Sixth Rangers went into Cabanatuan, took out the guards, and loaded up the POWs, Pajota and 120 Filipino warriors held a bridge against over 8,000 Japanese soldiers for more than an hour. At the end of the fighting, twenty-one Filipinos and four Americans had been killed, but they'd taken out 523 Japanese and rescued 511 American prisoners.

DOWN THE THROAT

The true unsung heroes of the American navy in the Pacific War were the gallant men of the Silent Service who launched daring submarine attacks against Japanese ships deep in enemy waters. Patrolling the coasts of enemy harbors and braving constant attacks from sub-killing destroyers and attack aircraft, US submarines thwarted enemy attempts to bring supplies, weapons, and reinforcements to the front lines. One of the most successful sub commanders was the awesomely named Slade Cutter, a square-jawed, six-foot-two All-American college football defensive tackle who wrote on his US Naval Academy application letter that his hobbies were "tobacco, swearing, and playing the flute." Operating in Tokyo Harbor and Okinawa, Cutter was famous for inventing the "down the throat" method of attacking, where the sub attacks his enemy head-on and, well, rams a torpedo down his throat. During six patrols commanding the USS *Pompano* and the USS *Seahorse*, Cutter accounted for twenty-three enemy ship kills, sending 142,300 tons of Japanese war matériel to the bottom of the Pacific. He received six medals for bravery during the war—one for each of his six long-range hunter-killer patrols.

KNOW YOUR VEHICLES

	USS *Johnston*	IJN *Yamato*
TYPE	*Fletcher*-class destroyer	*Yamato*-class superbattleship
COUNTRY	United States	Japan
COMMISSIONED	1943	1941
LENGTH	376 feet, 6 inches	862 feet, 10 inches
DISPLACEMENT	2,700 tons	64,170 tons
ARMOR	None	410 millimeters
ENGINE	Two geared steam turbines	Four steam turbines, four three-blade propellers
TOP SPEED	38 knots (44 mph)	27 knots (31 mph)
CREW	273	2,500
ARMAMENT	Five 5-inch cannons Ten 40mm torpedo tubes Seven 20mm antiaircraft cannons	Nine 18-inch cannons Twelve 6-inch cannons Twelve 5-inch cannons One hundred and thirty 25mm AA cannons

I think the stats here speak for themselves.

18

THE BATTLE OF THE BULGE

The Siege of Bastogne

December 16–26, 1944
Bastogne, Belgium

My men don't dig foxholes. Foxholes only slow up an offensive. Keep moving. We'll win this war, but we'll win it only by fighting and showing the Germans that we've got more guts than they have or ever will have.

—George S. Patton, in a speech to the US Third Army

JUST SIX MONTHS AFTER D-DAY, IT WAS already starting to look as if the German Army in the West was done for. Unyielding American troops were approaching the Rhine River toward Germany, British forces were surging north up the boot of Italy, and Russian tanks were rolling across Ukraine as quickly as their treads could carry them. Hitler was stretched too thin. He didn't have the manpower to defend his homeland on all three sides at the same time. All that was left was to drive into the heart of Germany.

With his back against the wall and his ambitious "kill every non-German person in the world" plans crumbling around him, Hitler decided it was time to bet it all on a last-ditch Hail Mary long bomb to change the ending of World War II. He committed the last of his reserve troops—all of them—to blitzing through the softest part of the American lines, crossing the Meuse River, capturing the Allied supply base at Antwerp, and cutting off or annihilating the entire British Twenty-First Army Group in Holland. If he could somehow maneuver Germany into a position of power against the Western Allies, maybe Britain and the United States would make peace and Hitler could dedicate all his energy to battling Russia. Sure, none of Hitler's top generals really thought this was a smart idea, a good use of resources, or even a little bit achievable, but it's not like he asked them anyway. So who cares?

Well, for some dumb reason the Americans didn't think Hitler would ever try to launch a massive tank attack through the Ardennes Forest (even though he'd already done this exact thing when he attacked France in 1940—go back to chapter 2 to read about this). So the troops stationed there were face-palmingly shocked on December 16, 1944, when they suddenly found themselves getting punched in the gut by the full weight of the German Fifth and Sixth Panzer Armies. Spearheaded by elite SS panzer troops under war-hardened veteran tank commander Joachim Peiper, a rampaging blitzkrieg of 250,000 men and 1,700 heavily armored Tiger and Panther tanks steamrolled through the snowy forest at top speed. These mighty war machines churned through the snow and underbrush, plowing down trees like bulldozers and ripping off 88mm cannon shots in every direction.

German troops advancing in the Ardennes Forest

American bazooka teams and Sherman tanks raced to react, but their shells simply bounced harmlessly off the armored hulls of the SS Tigers. Raw American recruits who had never seen combat before suddenly found themselves locked into a shooting match with SS veterans who had spent the last three and a half years ruthlessly blasting apart Russian tanks on the Eastern Front. Entire Allied divisions scattered, withdrew, surrendered, or simply ceased to exist. By the end of the first day, German panzers had carved a sixty-mile-deep gouge in the American battle lines. This section of land was now occupied by over twenty divisions of intimidating Nazi storm troopers, and it made a map of the war zone look all weird and lumpy. So when you're talking about the "Battle of the Bulge," it's not some annoying weight-loss reality TV series. It's a sixty-mile-long formation of armored Nazi tanks wasting dudes with machine guns.

The Americans didn't have much in the Ardennes sector at this time, so Supreme Allied Commander Dwight D. Eisenhower ordered the paratroopers of the 101st and Eighty-Second Airborne Divisions to hop into trucks and drive out to meet the panzers head-on. The Eighty-Second was sent to St. Vith, where these lightly armed guys could expect to take on Tiger tanks with their bare hands and maybe a bazooka or something, while the 101st was dispatched to a key city called Bastogne. Bastogne was important because if the Germans wanted to get to Antwerp (and they did), there were only seven roads that went there...and they all passed through Bastogne.

So under the command of Brigadier General Anthony McAuliffe, the 101st Airborne took up positions in Bastogne, dug foxholes in the freezing, ice-covered ground, cleared chest-high snowdrifts so they could have reasonable firing lines, and prepared to defend the city against pretty much the entire German Army at the same time. The 101st, known as the "Screamin' Eagles," arrived on the night of December 19. By dawn the next morning, they were completely surrounded by three divisions of German armored troops.

Paratroopers aren't really meant to defend cities against units like the elite German Panzer Lehr Division (one of the most experienced and deadliest tank units in the German military). They don't have the equipment or weapons. But these were some of the best and most experienced soldiers in the US Army, and they just happened to be camped out near the location of the German surprise attack, so now they had to figure out a way to slow down a huge enemy attack by any means necessary. Their efforts were heroic, but if there was to be any hope at all of stopping Hitler's assault, Eisenhower needed to get some tank-destroying reinforcements there in a hurry.

He called on his most trusted, toughest, and most hot-tempered commander: General George S. Patton.

Patton is a dude who is pretty much universally known as

one of the most ferocious men to ever wear the uniform of the United States Army. A no-nonsense, grumpy old warhorse who rocked a matching pair of ivory-handled cowboy revolvers and had a truly fantastic catalog of swear words, Patton was as hardcore as they get. He'd fought Pancho Villa's banditos in Mexico, driven a tank in World War I, defeated Rommel in North Africa, and once tried to shoot down a Messerschmitt with a pistol. People can say what they want about the man, but this was the dude to call when you wanted to *get things done*.

Patton's Third Army was deployed in battle in the Saar region, about 140 miles south of where this Bulge nonsense was going down, but he couldn't have cared less if you'd paid him. He told Ike he could have two divisions in Bastogne in two days. Eisenhower—and all the American and British officers in the room with him—looked at Patton as if he had lost his mind.

Then they gave him a chance to prove it.

Patton got to work with the sort of righteous determination that your grandpa uses to put together a new bike for you on Christmas morning. Driving straight out to the front lines, he went up and down to every one of his unit commanders, laying out the plan to get them disengaged, turned around, and moving north toward Bastogne as quickly as possible. There were Germans there who needed shooting, dang it, and by God his guys were going to be the ones doing the shooting.

Now, if you're going to call in the cavalry to ride to the rescue, you might as well ask a cavalryman. And Patton called on Lieutenant Colonel Creighton "Abe" Abrams, commander of the Fourth Armored Division's Thirty-Seventh Tank Battalion. Rolling at top speed down the ice-covered streets of Belgium, Abrams stood with the upper half of his body sticking out of his tank and a cigar sticking out of his mouth, plowing his Sherman through four feet of snow in temperatures of minus seven degrees Fahrenheit. A high school football captain from Springfield, Massachusetts, Colonel Abe was a former Seventh Cavalry officer who rode at the head of his columns and was famous among his men for always being in the middle of the most intense fighting in Europe. When his troops were getting waxed by Panther tanks outside the French town of Arracourt just a few days after D-Day, this guy drove his tank straight up to the closest enemy heavy tank and plastered it at point-blank range until it was a smoking hulk. By the time his pumped-up men were done, they'd destroyed an entire panzer regiment, even though they were driving weakly armored little M4 Sherman tanks that were way crappier than your standard German heavy tank. Now Abrams was riding hard through freezing temperatures in his newest M4, "Thunderbolt IV," calling out orders to his crew and preparing to race head-on into combat.

Back in Bastogne, the 101st were fighting for their lives. Hammered by enemy paratroopers, artillery, tanks, and

armored cars from every direction, the battered Americans struggled to hang on to their posts as ammunition dwindled and casualties mounted. Supported by a couple of tanks from the 10th Armored and a few guns from the African-American troops of the 333rd and 969th Field Artillery Battalions, the Screamin' Eagles laid down punishing fire against an enemy that outnumbered them five to one. It was so cold their canteens were freezing, men were losing fingers to frostbite, and rifles were getting jammed up with ice. The weather was cloudy and miserable, preventing any Allied airplanes from coming to help with supplies or bombing raids, and enemy assaults seemed to go on nonstop. Hitler's plan wouldn't work until the Nazis held Bastogne, and he wasn't going to rest until it had been pried from the cold, dead hands of the 101st Airborne Division.

Sixty miles away, Abe Abrams's column was rolling through a heavily defended German town, each tank firing its cannon and three machine guns at targets in every direction. Rocket-launcher-toting Nazi paratroopers popped out of cellars or opened fire from village windows just in time to be sprayed with .30-caliber machine-gun fire. Gigantic Panther and Tiger II tanks (more on these at the end of the chapter) blasted at Abrams's Shermans, knowing they could waste a US tank with just a single round from their colossal cannons, but the Americans fearlessly drove head-on to engage them, with two Shermans distracting them from the front while another drove around in a flanking move to nail the Tiger in its lightly armored sides or back.

On December 22, General McAuliffe of the 101st Airborne in Bastogne received a pretty long letter from the German commander, asking him to surrender the town or be destroyed. McAuliffe's reply was just one word: *Nuts!* Then he handed the paper back to the German messenger. The dude looked at it, didn't understand, and asked McAuliffe's aide to define *nuts*.

The aide looked the German in the eye and said, "It means go to hell."

Four days and nights of nonstop driving and shooting had reduced Colonel Abe's command from seventy tanks to just twenty-one, but they continued, fighting for every inch of the frozen countryside, clearing a path through the Germans so the rest of Patton's tanks could surge forward. They'd covered 140 miles in four days, an insane accomplishment considering that the roads were covered in two inches of black ice and lined with Nazi antitank cannons.

Just after dark on December 26, 1944, the lead tanks from Colonel Abe's Thirty-Seventh Tank Battalion rolled up to a man in an American uniform. The badge on his sleeve was from the 101st Airborne.

Before General McAuliffe met with Colonel Abe Abrams at

American soldiers in the Ardennes Forest

ten that night, he ordered his men to shave, wash their faces, and get their uniforms in order. He didn't want those showboat tank boys to think the 101st Airborne Division needed any flashy cavalry to come "rescue" them from a good fight.

More and more reinforcements rolled into Bastogne. The relief of the city was George S. Patton's finest hour. In just four days, he'd disengaged the entire Third Army from battle, turned it ninety degrees north, and run it 150 miles through ice, narrow roads, and frozen snow to slam the Germans in the flank. As more and more troops surged into the pocket, Hitler

General Creighton Abrams's M4A3E8 Sherman tank

knew the battle was lost. Bastogne had held. St. Vith had held. The SS panzers withdrew intact, but the last armored reserves of Germany were no longer an effective attacking force. It would be less than three months before American forces were driving across the Rhine River into Germany.

To this day, if you visit Bastogne, the center of downtown is known as McAuliffe Square. Colonel Abe Abrams, a two-time Distinguished Service Cross recipient for bravery under fire in World War II, went on to serve in Korea, to be part of the occupation army in Germany, and to become the overall commander of all US troops in the Vietnam War. Nowadays the frontline main battle tank of the American army is known as the M1A1 Abrams in his honor.

THE FIRST CRUISE MISSILES

Starting in June 1944, the Germans began launching V-bombs, which were basically the world's first cruise missiles. Fired from sites in Holland, France, and Belgium toward targets in England, V-1 and V-2 rockets were basically just huge bombs strapped to jet fuel and guided by a preset internal compass. The most feared of these was the V-2, which was a forty-six-foot-long missile tipped with 2,150 pounds of explosives that could accelerate to speeds of over three thousand miles an hour. Thousands of V-bombs were fired at London, Manchester, and surrounding cities during the war. Most hit their targets, but about a third either crashed because of equipment failure or were shot down by AA guns or RAF Spitfire pilots.

TO HELL AND BACK

The most decorated American soldier in World War II was Lieutenant Audie Murphy. A clean-cut kid from Texas, Murphy was a beast on the battlefield, and when he captured an enemy machine-gun nest in Italy, he picked up the gun, fired it from his hip like an action movie hero, and took out two other positions with it. Later, in the Holtzwihr Forest in January 1945, he took on 250 German infantry and six tanks all by himself. With the rest of his unit wiped out, Murphy ran over to a burned-out M-10 tank destroyer, jumped onto the back of it, and started shooting the .50-caliber machine gun from an exposed position. He kept shooting for over an hour. He wiped out a battalion of Germans, then used the tank's radio to call in artillery strikes on the panzers. After the war, he returned to the States and starred in the movie about his life, *To Hell and Back*.

WHO'S ON FIRST?

To help spread confusion and chaos during the attack in the Ardennes, the Germans dressed up a bunch of English-speaking guys in captured American uniforms and sent them behind US lines to assassinate officers, secure bridges, and give misleading intelligence reports to officers. Rolling around in US jeeps, these guys even did obnoxious stuff like change road signs and give bad directions to tank drivers. The Americans got around this by setting up checkpoints where military police would quiz guys about things like major-league baseball and American geography.

KNOW YOUR VEHICLES

	M4A1 Sherman	PzKpfw. VIB Tiger II
TYPE	Medium tank	Heavy tank
COUNTRY	United States	Germany
FIRST PRODUCED	1942	1944
LENGTH	19 feet, 2 inches	24 feet, 3 inches
WEIGHT	33 tons	76 tons
ARMOR	75 millimeters	150 millimeters
ENGINE	400-hp Continental R975 radia	690-hp Maybach HL 230 V-12 gasoline
TOP SPEED	25 mph	24 mph
CREW	5	5
ARMAMENT	One 75mm M3 L/40 cannon Two .30-caliber machine guns One .50-caliber machine gun	One 88mm KwK 43 L/71 cannon Two 7.92mm machine guns

The newest German heavy tank was the *Königstiger,* which means "Bengal tiger" in German but always gets translated to *Tiger II* in English (because *könig* is the German word for "king"). Whatever you want to call it, this thing was big, mean, and scary and had a humongous cannon that could one-shot anything in the American arsenal. The American M4s were agile and quick, but more important, there were way more of them—the United States built 49,234 Shermans during World War II and the Germans only had 492 Tiger IIs, which were also prone to breakdowns. They were very complicated pieces of equipment that required tons of resources to repair after battles.

19

THE FALL OF BERLIN

Germany's Last Stand

Berlin, Germany
April 30, 1945

The Soviets battled the German soldiers and drafted civilians street by street until we could hear explosions and rifle fire right in our immediate vicinity. As the noise got closer, we could even hear the horrible guttural screaming of the Soviet soldiers, which sounded to us like enraged animals. Shots shattered our windows and shells exploded in our garden, and suddenly the Soviets were on our street.

—Dorothea von Schwanenfluegel, Berlin resident

THE WAR HAD FINALLY COME TO THE STREETS of Berlin.

With a triumphant swagger, the tramping boots of 2.5 million Russian soldiers now shook the rubble-strewn streets of the German capital. These were street fighters, veterans of brutal slugfests in Leningrad, Moscow, and Stalingrad, and dozens of other grueling battles across Poland and eastern Germany. And they were laying waste to the once-proud city, clearing it of resistance street by street. Supported by forty-one thousand artillery cannons, six thousand tanks, and sixty-five hundred bomber aircraft, the men

A Berlin street demolished in the fighting, 1945

and women of the Red Army pounded the heart of the German Reich. Infantry with submachine guns and rifles advanced under the cover of smoke grenades. T-34s fired point-blank into apartment buildings to level Nazi sniper nests. Katyusha rocket launcher trucks unleashed barrages of explosives by the dozen. Heck, the Soviets had even brought machine gun–equipped motorboats to put in the river.

In their way were just a couple hundred thousand heavily outnumbered, demoralized, and outmatched Germans. These guys made up the *Volkssturm*, which sounds all cool and everything because it's German for "People's Storm," but in reality it was just a disorganized group of teenage boys, old men in their sixties, and Berlin city police officers who had been thrown together to try to stop the entire might of the Soviet Union. Fighting in regular street clothes and using outdated rifles from the World War I era, these makeshift troops did everything they could to defend their homes. They barricaded streets, laid out barbed wire, set land mines, and hid machine guns in overturned streetcars.

At the heart of the city, in his bombproof bunker deep beneath the garden of the Reich Chancellery, Adolf Hitler stubbornly clung to the last remaining shreds of his empire. Hiding out with his girlfriend, Eva Braun; his dog, Blondi (a German shepherd, of course); and a few trusted generals, the leader of Nazi Germany attempted to strategize victory as he ordered insane counterattacks that could never happen.

He held on to the delusion that the German Twelfth Army would disengage frontline American forces sixty miles away and come running over to Berlin to save him, and when his commanders told him he was nuts, he just yelled at them a lot and then fired them for being idiots.

The fighting above was converging on the Reichstag Building. Erected in 1894, this was a domed concrete government building several stories high that was home to the lower parliament of the German congress and was the traditional capitol of Germany. It was here in 1933 that a fire had allowed Hitler to seize power and crush his political enemies. Now it was the symbolic heart of his rapidly disintegrating Reich, defended by the final grim remnants of his elite SS soldiers. For the Russians, final victory in World War II would come only when a red Soviet flag was flying from the roof.

Knowing full well that this was their last stand, the SS turned the Reichstag into a fortress. These fanatical warriors were determined to make sure the Soviets paid in blood for every inch of land they gained. Five thousand men from the SS, the Hitler Youth (basically Nazi Boy Scouts), and cadets from the Berlin Naval Academy bricked up the doors, cut loopholes for machine guns, overturned buses to serve as barricades, and fortified the over four-hundred-yard-wide plaza with flooded ditches, antitank trenches, sandbag machine-gun nests, and even a couple of 88mm antiaircraft flak artillery cannons.

At four AM on April 30, 1945, the men of the Red Army's

150th Rifle Division, Seventy-Ninth Rifle Corps, Third Shock Army, were given orders to storm the Reichstag. The attack began with an artillery bombardment from Katyusha rocket trucks and epic 220mm artillery guns, raining down missiles and explosives and anticoncrete bombs on enemy positions just a few hundred yards ahead of the main Soviet lines. Under the cover of the explosions and smoke, screaming Red Army troops ran toward the main gate of the Reichstag, drawing heavy fire from trenches, sniper shots from the windows, and point-blank cannon shots from SS artillery gunners. Across the plaza, machine-gun nests opened up from the Kroll Opera House, a place where composers like Strauss and Wagner once put on classical music concerts. The guns were silenced only after a Soviet artillery cannon three miles away dropped a 540-pound shell on the building that blasted a crater measuring thirty feet across. The Ministry of the Interior, home to Germany's infamous Gestapo secret police, suffered a similar fate.

Explosions also raked the Red Army lines, driving the Russians back with heavy losses. The unrelenting Russians came on again at eleven thirty AM, though, and again at one PM, both times being hammered by hellacious fire. The SS shot bazookas from third-story windows, hurled grenades from the trenches, and even called in mortar fire from a cannon position in the Berlin Zoo a few hundred yards away. The last Tiger tanks in the German arsenal drove up onto the lawn outside the capitol, firing heavy 88mm shells into the Russian lines and spraying bullets from their three machine guns.

Now, here's a weird thing that happened. During the attack at one PM, some Russian dude remarked that he thought he'd seen a red banner hanging from the Reichstag. He hadn't. In fact, the Russians hadn't been within two hundred yards of the front door of the place, so whatever the heck this guy saw was some kind of hallucination. Unfortunately, someone reported this sighting to Marshal Georgy Zhukov, commanding officer of the Russian army in Berlin, who got so pumped about the whole thing that he called Stalin on the phone to tell him what was up. Stalin then broadcast the victory on the radio to every single person in the Soviet Union. The story was picked up on Western radio, and by two thirty every human being on earth thought there was a red banner flying from the German Reichstag.

Then someone told Zhukov, "Well, no, that's not actually a hundred percent true."

Now, Stalin wasn't the sort of totalitarian dictator who would be cool with the idea of looking like an idiot in front of the entire world, and he *was* the kind of guy who would have a commander or two executed for something like this. So Zhukov freaked out and ordered his men to have a red banner hanging from the roof of the Reichstag at some point on April 30, 1945, or he was going to personally start punching people.

So, at six PM, the men of the 150th Rifle Division were ordered to capture the building no matter what. Racing through the smoke and dust and fire, the ferocious might of the Red Army stormed their way across the bridge into the plaza while Soviet artillery dropped explosives just a few hundred feet in front of them. The Russians ran through minefields, charged into trenches, and drove T-34 tanks right up to the front door to shoot down the bricked-up entrance. Battle-hardened men of the Soviet Union shouldered through the thick iron doors, racing into the main hallway of the German government, where members of the parliament had once debated and given speeches. From the second floor, four hundred SS storm troopers rained fire and grenades down on the Russians, defending their government building with unbridled fury. Above the senate floor, the white dome of the Reichstag roared in flames, sprinkling burning rafters and broken glass down on the assaulting Russians.

The Soviets suffered badly, but these tenacious fighters hadn't come so close to victory only to be turned back now. These were veteran men and women who had survived bloody fighting across the Eastern Front and watched their homes and cities burned and their families killed by invading German soldiers. They had liberated concentration camps, survived sieges, and witnessed the horrors of Nazi brutality up close and personal. The last thing on their mind was mercy or compassion. They wanted revenge.

The Reichstag after the battle, 1945

Leading a small squad of men, Captain Stepan Neustroev of the First Battalion, 756th Rifle Regiment, led his men down the wood-paneled hallways of the Reichstag's second floor. Every room was barricaded and full of Nazis, but this veteran officer had already been wounded twice in this war and wasn't afraid of something as insignificant as a dozen Germans with machine guns trying to kill him. Shooting through doors, climbing over barricades, and clearing rooms

with hand grenades, Neustroev and his men raced through the burning building, fighting for every step. At ten thirty PM, four hours after they'd entered, Neustroev and his squad were on the roof of the German Reichstag. One of his men climbed onto a statue of Kaiser Wilhelm, the German leader during World War I, and planted a large red Soviet banner high above the war-torn streets of Berlin.

In his bunker, less than a mile away, the leader of Germany knew his twelve-year reign was finally at an end. As enemy troops closed in, Adolf Hitler married his girlfriend, then poisoned his dog, and then he and Eva killed themselves—her by poison, him by shooting himself with the same kind of gun James Bond carries. Hitler's men carried his body out into the garden and set it on fire to keep the Russians from being able to parade it around. Hitler was ten days away from his fifty-sixth birthday.

The Germans kept fighting around Berlin, but at 2:41 AM on May 7, 1945, the last remnants of the German Army signed an official agreement of unconditional surrender. The war in Europe was finally over.

RAISING THE FLAG

Perhaps the most iconic photo of World War II is the picture of five US Marines and a US Navy corpsman raising an American flag atop Mount Suribachi on the Japanese island of Iwo Jima. When the Marine Corps stormed the island in early 1945, they had to fight their way with fire and steel through 22,000 fanatical enemy soldiers who battled until nearly every single one of them was dead. At the height of the battle, men from the Fifth Marine Division reached the summit of the rocky mountain dominating the island and raised the flag to show their comrades it was now under Marine control. The photo, taken by Pulitzer Prize–winning photographer Joe Rosenthal on February 23, 1945, created such a powerful feeling among Americans that the Soviet Union decided it would be a great propaganda move to totally borrow that idea and take a selfie with the Red Flag over the Reichstag. So, well after the actual raising of the flag, a couple of Russians staged their own version of it, and, as expected, the picture is now the defining photo of the Battle for Berlin.

COMMISSARS

Most Red Army units were joined by a Communist Party political officer known as a commissar, who would fight with them on the battlefield. The commissar held a rank equal to the commander of the unit, and it was his job to lecture the soldiers on the wonders of the Communist Party and their glorious struggle against global Nazism, usually by yelling pump-up words of encouragement during battle and then pulling his pistol and shooting any Soviet soldier who tried to run away from the battle. Hitler, as you can expect, wasn't too fond of these guys, and he had a standing order in the German Army that any captured Red Army political officers were to be executed on sight (they were easy to identify because they wore really cool-looking hats), an order that was routinely ignored by many German officers.

KNOW YOUR VEHICLES

	Panzer 1000 Landkreuzer *Ratte*	Iosef Stalin IS-2
TYPE	Superheavy tank	Heavy tank
COUNTRY	Germany	Soviet Union
FIRST PRODUCED	N/A	1943
LENGTH	115 feet	20 feet, 4 inches
WEIGHT	1,000+ tons	51 tons
ARMOR	360 millimeters	120 millimeters
ENGINE	Eight Daimler-Benz U-boat engines, 17,000 hp	600-hp V-2 12-cylinder diesel
TOP SPEED	25 mph	23 mph
CREW	20+	4
ARMAMENT	Two 280mm SK C/34 naval cannons; one 128mm KwK 44 L/55 cannon; eight 20mm FlaK-38 antiaircraft guns; two 15mm MG 151/15 autocannons	One 122mm D25-T cannon Two 7.62mm machine guns

When the war started turning against him, Hitler approved designs to create an insane video game–style "land battleship" that would be powered by four U-boat engines, require a crew of forty guys, and weigh so much that it would destroy any road you tried to drive it on. At 115 feet, the interior of the tank would have been bigger than a regulation NBA basketball court, and was supposed to have a sick bay, a bathroom, sleeping quarters, and storage for two BMW motorcycles. It had twin naval cannons on the front that could fire a four-hundred-pound shell a distance of twenty-five miles, and also had various other cannons and guns mounted in every direction. For comparison, I've put it next to the Russian IS-2, a massively successful Tiger-killing tank so awesome that Stalin named it after himself. The Panzer 1000 was never actually produced, but those wacky Germans did build the turret for it just to see what would happen. They ended up using it as a coastal defense naval battery in Norway.

20

TYPHOON OF STEEL

The Battle for Okinawa

April 1–June 22, 1945
Okinawa, Empire of Japan

The time of the attack has finally come. I have my doubts as to whether this all-out offensive will succeed, but I will fight fiercely with the thought in mind that this war for the Empire will last 100 years.

—Unidentified Japanese infantryman,
Imperial Thirty-Second Army

THE LAST BATTLE OF WORLD WAR II WAS fought by United States Marines assaulting an old-school moat to get into a medieval samurai castle on Japanese soil.

After months of bitter island-hopping battles all the way across the Pacific, the United States had finally reached the last stop in its campaign to bring the war to the Emperor's doorstep. Technically part of Japan itself, the rocky island of Okinawa is sixty miles long, with a harbor and an airfield that would be the perfect jumping-off point for an all-out amphibious attack on the Japanese home islands and Tokyo itself. The only real problem with the place was that it was home to about a hundred and twenty thousand high-octane Japanese warriors who had sworn a blood oath to defend it with their last breath.

It was before dawn on April 1, 1945—a date that was both April Fools' Day and Easter Sunday. Japanese scouts looked on in horror at a seven-mile-wide sea of landing craft that stormed toward the shores off the coast of Okinawa. Over the course of several hours, the men of the Tenth US Army and the First and Sixth US Marine Divisions hit the beaches on a fleet of 1,760 landing craft and 700 DUKW "ducks" (those big weird-looking truck/boat things that take up two lanes on the highway and give out expensive guided tours in some American cities), and there wasn't much the defenders could do to stop them.

From his cool-looking underground base in a hand-dug cave deep beneath Shuri Castle, Lieutenant General Mitsuru Ushijima prepared his defenses. The former commandant of the Japanese Military Academy, Ushijima had fought the Communists during the Russian Revolution in 1918, battled Chinese guerrillas in the Gobi Desert, and gone sword-to-sword with the Brits in Burma. Now he commanded the largest, most powerful, and best-equipped force of Japanese defenders the Americans would ever face: sixty-seven thousand men from the battle-tested Thirty-Second Army, supported by nine thousand Imperial Japanese Navy troops who'd only come on land when they misplaced their boats at the bottom of the ocean. He was supported by forty thousand ragtag militiamen recruited from the local population, a number that included the "Lily Corps." This brave group of local high school girls had volunteered to dig bullets out of wounded soldiers and to stitch up their wounds on the front lines of the battle.

A hardened student of war, Ushijima had studied all the previous American attacks on Japanese islands, had learned his enemy's tactics, and prepared to defend the island accordingly. His men had spent months digging a massive network of tunnels and caves through the mountains, using nothing more than shovels and pickaxes. These positions were well hidden; loaded with bullets, medical supplies, and food; and completely protected against bombing runs from B-17s and artillery shells lobbed onto them from American battleships offshore. Ushijima had presited his artillery, hidden machine-gun nests and tunnel entrances, and dug fortified bunkers at key positions. He was pretty sure he couldn't stop the "typhoon of steel" coming at him, but he was going to see this through to the bloody end the way any good samurai would.

Almost immediately after the landings began, the Americans encountered a new kind of foe: the kamikaze. With few experienced pilots left in their ranks, the Japanese basically decided, "Well, forget shooting and dropping bombs, let's just get a bunch of crazy dudes to get into fighter planes loaded with bombs and crash them into American ships. Flying in sizable waves and clusters of two or three at a time, ultrapatriotic Japanese pilots slammed their airplanes head-on into US landing craft and warships. They came at the Americans in stripped-down Zeros, old-school wooden biplanes, and a new, ultradeadly weapon known as the "Cherry Blossom," which is basically a human-controlled missile. These horrible things were dropped from Japanese bombers like an actual bomb, but with a pilot attached. Once dropped, the kamikaze turned on the rocket engine and accelerated to six hundred miles an hour toward US ships while strapped to forty-five hundred pounds of explosive with no ejection seat. Ship gunners scanned the skies, and Marine Corps and Navy F4U Corsair fighter planes were constantly on patrol to try

The USS *Bunker Hill* burning after a kamikaze attack

to shoot down incoming enemy craft, but despite their heroic efforts, the navy was still losing something like one ship a day to enemy suicide attacks.

Another example of how desperate the Japanese were to defend their homeland came on April 7, 1945, when they launched their superbattleship the *Yamato* in Operation Ten-Go. The *Yamato*, the 72,000-ton warship that had faced off against Taffy-3 back in chapter 17, launched from mainland Japan. Its mission was simple—sail into Okinawa harbor, open fire with its eighteen-inch cannons and 145 machine guns, and fight until destroyed.

The mission didn't go so hot—an American sub spotted the *Yamato* shortly after it left the harbor, and US airplanes smashed it almost immediately. The biggest surface warship in history was nailed with seven bombs and twelve torpedoes before erupting in an enormous explosion and slipping beneath the waves. No halfway-sane navy in the world would bother building another battleship like this one.

Back on the ground in the mud and dust of Okinawa, the Americans were finally getting their first taste of what Ushijima had in store for them. Resistance had been light in the northern part of the island, but when the Americans headed south, they were lit up by Japanese artillery and hidden machine-gun nests the second they stepped out into the open. The battlefront was a five-mile-wide stretch centered on the heights overlooking the curved roofs and cool-looking

A US Marine attacking an enemy position on Okinawa

torii gates of towering Shuri Castle. The ancient home to samurai kings of Okinawa, Shuri Castle had a moat and defensive walls that had been updated for the twentieth century with machine-gun nests, antivehicle trenches, mortar pits, concrete bunkers, minefields, hidden artillery and sniper positions, and literally tens of miles of underground tunnels and secret passages that were perfect for launching deadly ambushes. American soldiers would bravely surge ahead, wipe out an enemy machine-gun nest, and then turn around only to see a trapdoor pop open and a cranky Japanese dude with an assault rifle and a stick of dynamite running out after them.

General Ushijima's plan was to turtle up and harass the American forces with constant surprise attacks, sniper raids, and other annoying, ambush-type tactics. But let's be honest here: Holing up in a cave taking potshots at guys isn't really the way the ancient samurai liked to do things. And before long, all this fight, hide, retreat, sneak attack nonsense started to get on the nerves of Ushijima's top assistant, Major General Isamu Cho. Cho was an old-school warrior who was basically ripped out of a samurai castle in the seventeenth century and dropped boots-first into the middle of World War II. This hotheaded, attack-first, glory-or-death warmonger carried a full-on katana samurai sword with him at all times (many Japanese officers did this); and when he'd had a little too much whiskey to drink, he apparently would do a really intense "sword dance" in the middle of a strategy meeting. I don't really know what the heck this would look like, but let's just assume it was as awesome as I'm imagining it to be.

Cho was a banzai war hawk who had participated in a military coup against the Japanese government in the early 1930s because he didn't think the parliament was hardcore enough. He personally challenged a Soviet commander to a sword fight during battles in Manchuria, commanded an infantry unit against British soldiers in Burma, and was one of the Japanese officers in charge of the attack on Shanghai at the very beginning of the war and this book. This guy was not the sort of man who sat back and waited for the enemy, and he eventually convinced Ushijima that it was time to launch a counteroffensive.

In the early-morning hours of May 4, 1945, Cho and several battalions of the Thirty-Second Army opened up on the American frontline infantry with a barrage from hundreds of artillery cannons and mortars, rushing out of their bunkers with bayonets at the ready in a glorious banzai charge. While his guys locked into hand-to-hand combat with American army soldiers, Cho also sent a unit of combat engineers in boats to sail around and attack the Americans from the rear and set a bunch of bombs behind US lines. But that kind of went sideways when the First Marine Division saw what was going on and leveled the enemy transports with artillery and machine-gun fire while they were still out in the water. The head-on attack was beaten back after ruthless up-close fighting, without accomplishing nearly what Cho had hoped.

Bloodied, dirty, covered in mud, and getting nailed by torrential rains, the Americans fought on. It was the middle of May. Hitler was dead. Germany had surrendered. Infantrymen were coming home from Normandy as heroes. US president Franklin D. Roosevelt had died and been replaced by his vice president, Harry S. Truman. Yet for the Marines and soldiers on Okinawa, there was still work to do.

The battle for Shuri Castle was some of the most brutal fighting of the entire war. American forces rolled up Sherman tanks specially outfitted with flamethrowers to incinerate bunkers and smoke out defenders. High-explosive satchel bombs were dropped into tunnels to blast them until they collapsed. Bulldozers came up to level bunkers and block in caves. Avenger and Corsair fighter-bomber aircraft were strafing ground targets, and men on the front lines were radioing in coordinates for offshore battleships to open fire with huge sixteen-inch concrete-piercing rounds. On Sugar Loaf Hill overlooking the castle, the men of the Sixth Marine Division sprinted uphill with bayonets and knives in what their commander referred to as "a banzai charge of our own," overrunning an enemy whose hyperdeveloped and stubborn sense of honor refused to allow them to retreat or surrender.

US Marines fighting on Okinawa, 1945

US Army divisions ferociously fought their way through the pouring rain into the outer fortifications of Shuri Castle, picking off snipers with flamethrowers and turning back enemy bayonet attacks every step of the way.

On May 29, the sun came out for the first time in weeks. The men of the First Battalion, Fifth Marine Regiment, First Marine Division, moved out toward Shuri Castle, battling their way through the moat and over the walls of the once-proud samurai fortress. Surrounded by crumbling columns, blasted-in roofs, and shredded Zen gardens, the Marines ripped off fire with M1 rifles, Colt .45 handguns, and heavy .30-caliber machine guns, clearing out the enemy step by step. Then, around midday, the men of Company A forced their way into the main courtyard of Shuri Castle, climbed to the roof, and flew a flag triumphantly from the top of the castle.

Of course, it's worth mentioning that the commander of Company A, Captain Julian Dusenbury, was a South Carolina boy, and the flag his company flew up there was a Confederate battle flag from the Civil War.

The commander of the American Tenth Army was Lieutenant General Simon Bolivar Buckner Jr. Buckner's dad, Simon Bolivar Buckner Sr., was the Confederate commander who had surrendered Fort Donelson to Ulysses S. Grant in the American Civil War. But this guy wasn't in the mood for jokes. He told Dusenbury that this wasn't about North or South or anything like that—every man there was an American, and that was what they were fighting for. He replaced the flag with the Stars and Stripes two days later.

Lieutenant General Mitsuru Ushijima had withdrawn from Shuri when he lost the heights overlooking the castle and was now holed up a few miles south with the shattered remnants of his army. Bloody, hopelessly outnumbered, and in an impossible position, he received a letter from his counterpart, General Buckner. He, like Ushijima, had been commandant of his country's top military academy. Both men had come up with the infantry. Now Buckner was asking Ushijima, man to man, soldier to soldier, to surrender his command and end this needless bloodshed.

Ushijima laughed when he read it. A samurai does not surrender.

The fighting would continue for another couple of weeks as Ushijima desperately held out. On June 18, 1945, Simon Bolivar Buckner Jr. was killed by an enemy mortar while surveying the front lines. He would be the highest-ranking American officer of World War II to die in combat.

Three days later, just five miles from where General Buckner was killed, Generals Ushijima and Cho knew it was all over. With American forces storming their base, the two modern-day samurai warriors prepared to go out with honor by committing ritual suicide, known as seppuku. Cho donned traditional samurai clothing. Ushijima put on his military dress uniform. As enemy grenades rumbled around them, the Japanese commanders kneeled on tatami mats, drew their *tanto* daggers, and stabbed themselves in the stomach, cutting across their bellies according to tradition. They were then beheaded by their aides.

The United States ended up with 16,000 Marines, 23,000 soldiers, and 10,000 sailors dead, wounded, or missing in the Battle for Okinawa. Thirty-three ships were sunk. Another 350 were damaged. For the Japanese, it was somehow worse—of the 120,000 Japanese soldiers defending the island, 110,000 died. The rest were taken prisoner only because they were too badly wounded to continue fighting or kill themselves. A third of the

civilian population of the island was dead; a large number of those were people who killed themselves because the Japanese government made up a bunch of lies about how the Americans would eat their babies and enslave them and do other horrible stuff. Very few buildings of any kind were left standing.

It was a truly horrible sight, but in the minds of many American troops on the ground, this was just a taste of things to come. If this was the cost of taking Okinawa, how much devastation would come from an invasion of the Japanese home islands themselves?

THE ATOMIC BOMB

I have no regrets. I think we did right, and we couldn't have done it differently. Yeah, I know it has been suggested the second bomb, Nagasaki, was not necessary. The guys who cry on shoulders. When you are in a war to the death I don't think you stand around and ask, "Is it right?"

—Leona Woods, the only female scientist to work on the Manhattan Project

The American military had seen the devastation at Okinawa, Iwo Jima, and dozens of other islands across the Pacific. The soldiers and Marines had suffered tremendously storming those bases, taking large numbers of casualties in the face of horrible attacks like banzai charges and kamikaze assaults. The Japanese did not surrender, and they were all ready to give their lives for the Emperor.

All that remained was the Japanese homeland, and by all accounts it would see the bloodiest and most horrific fighting of the entire war. The Japanese government, spreading propaganda as they had in Okinawa, told citizens that when the Americans attacked, every Japanese man, woman, and child would be given a bamboo spear and a hand grenade and ordered to fight back until killed. Initial estimates suggested US casualties of close to a million, with the end result being something very close to the complete extermination of Japanese civilization.

But maybe there was another way.

Throughout the war, American scientists, physicists, and engineers had been working on a top secret, super-high-tech weapon that harnessed the power of nuclear fission to create an explosion unlike anything this side of the sun's surface. Coordinated by Army Colonel Leslie R. Groves, the engineer who built the Pentagon, this operation was known as the Manhattan Project. Supersecret research labs across the country were straining every resource to create and use weaponized uranium and plutonium isotopes. A lab in Oak Ridge, Tennessee, discovered and produced uranium-238 molecules. Another one in Berkeley, California, made plutonium. In Chicago, a research team assembled a pile of fissionable material underneath the bleachers in an old baseball stadium and created the first controlled nuclear reaction.

And, finally, at the base in Los Alamos, New Mexico, research teams under physicist J. Robert Oppenheimer put it all together. On July 16, 1945, at Trinity, an isolated corner of the Alamogordo Bombing and Gunnery Range, the first nuclear bomb was successfully test-fired. It was unlike anything anyone had ever seen: destruction on an immense, unprecedented scale.

President Roosevelt died of a stroke on April 12, 1945, and was succeeded by his vice president, Harry S. Truman. Truman reviewed two reports: the American military operational plan for the land invasion of Japan, and Oppenheimer's report on the effectiveness of the atomic bomb. No matter what decision he made, hundreds of thousands of people were going to die on his order.

On August 6, 1945, a B-29 Superfortress known as *Enola Gay* released a uranium-238 atomic bomb from the atmosphere high above the Japanese port city of Hiroshima. The bomb detonated a few hundred yards above the ground, erupting into a white-hot bolt of flame that incinerated every single thing in a five-mile radius. It left behind nothing more than a pile of ash and a towering mushroom cloud that blew so high it almost knocked *Enola Gay* out of the air. Sixty-six thousand Japanese people, mostly civilians, were vaporized. Another seventy thousand were wounded. Tens of thousands more would suffer from radiation sickness over the next decade.

In the blink of an eye, a single bomb had killed more people than Robert E. Lee had brought to the Battle of Gettysburg.

Three days later, the United States did it again.

This time the target was Nagasaki, another semi-military town in the south of Japan. Another sixty-four thousand people (again, mostly unarmed civilians) were killed or wounded outright, vaporized into ash or burned to death by extreme radiation. The city was flattened. Extreme heat from the detonation fused sand and dirt into a glass-filled crater. For weeks after the bombing, people continued to die of radiation poisoning, burns, and other wounds suffered during the attack. Even in 1985, forty years after the bomb dropped, rates of cancer, leukemia, and birth defects were significantly higher in Nagasaki than in other cities throughout Japan.

The Emperor of Japan ordered his people to surrender. Less than a month later, General Douglas MacArthur oversaw the official signing of the surrender documents aboard the American battleship USS *Missouri*. World War II had finally come to an end.

Since the United States Army hadn't been certain what decision Truman would make, they'd ordered the production of Purple Heart awards to be given out to American troops killed or wounded in the invasion of Japan. These medals were produced and stored in a warehouse in Arlington, Virginia, but ultimately weren't needed because Truman chose to drop the bomb instead.

In the seventy years that have passed since World War II, the United States has fought wars in Korea, Vietnam, Somalia, Grenada, and Afghanistan, and in Iraq twice. To this day, when a soldier, Marine, airman, or sailor is wounded in combat, they are issued a medal from this warehouse.

KNOW YOUR VEHICLES

	Vought F4U-1A Corsair	Yokosuka MXY7 Ohka
TYPE	Fighter aircraft	Kamikaze aircraft
COUNTRY	United States	Japan
FIRST PRODUCED	1943	1945
LENGTH	33 feet, 4 inches	19 feet, 11 inches
WEIGHT	11,093 pounds	4,718 pounds
ENGINE	2,000-hp Pratt & Whitney R-2800-8 radial	Three Type 4 Model 20 rocket motors
RATE OF CLIMB	3,250 feet per minute	N/A
TOP SPEED	417 mph	650 mph
CREW	1	1
ARMAMENT	Six .50-caliber machine guns Four 5-inch rockets	One 2,646-pound bomb

By 1945 Japanese Zeros had long been outclassed by Navy Hellcats and Marine Corsairs, but in the skies above Okinawa the US Marine Corps had its hands full trying to take out the Ohka "Cherry Blossom" kamikaze rockets as they streaked toward their targets. The Ohka was just a bomb with a guy (who wouldn't survive) driving it, and its huge speed and small size made it very difficult to hit. Marine Corps Corsair pilots did an admirable job, however, and their planes were so responsive, successful, and beloved that they would continue to be in service throughout the Korean War in 1950.

CONCLUSION

Today the guns are silent. A great tragedy has ended. A great victory has been won. The skies no longer rain with death. The seas bear only commerce. Men everywhere walk upright in the sunlight. The entire world lies quietly at peace.

—General of the Army Douglas MacArthur,
Supreme Commander for the Allied Powers

WORLD WAR II INVOLVED HUNDREDS OF MILlions of people from every corner of the globe and changed our history forever. Humanity went into the conflict flying around on old-school canvas airplanes and came out of it with jet fighters and nuclear weapons. We invented radar, sonar, synthetic fuel, and rubber, and we were very close to harnessing nuclear energy. We saw the greatest and purest forms of heroism, and we saw the absolute blackest evil.

So what happened next?

Well, the first order of business was to ensure that something like this never, ever, ever (and I mean *ever*) happened again. In October 1945, just two months after the surrender of Japan, fifty-one countries created the United Nations, an international organization in which countries try to work out their problems before they just start shooting and blowing things up. The effectiveness of the United Nations is argued about a lot, sure, but today 191 countries are involved and we haven't had a World War III yet. So let's call it a win.

The United Nations was headed up by the two countries that emerged from World War II as the strongest nations on earth: the United States and the Soviet Union. Neither country was really a mega–global power in 1939, but by the end of the war they were both highly industrialized powerhouses with plenty of money and a bunch of guns and tanks and things. So naturally they distrusted each other and started talking smack and being all suspicious, which started a US-Russian mutual dislike that extends to this day. At its height, this international staring contest was known as the Cold War, and even though no bullets were ever officially fired in anger between the two countries, they did come scarily close to annihilating the earth with nuclear weapons on more than one occasion.

Britain and France were okay after the war, but it was obvious that those nations' days of running globe-spanning empires were coming to an end. The British Empire split up, and British forces moved out of places across the Middle East, Asia, and Africa. India gained its independence and split into India and Pakistan in 1948. That same year, the United Nations agreed to divide British Palestine up into two regions: One would remain the home of the Palestinian people (who were mostly Muslims), and one would be a new homeland for the Jewish people who had suffered so monumentally at the hands of Hitler's death squads. Jews from Europe and around the world flocked to the new land of Israel, their people's ancient homeland, and while this was great for the Jews, it kind of ticked off the Palestinian people who were already living there. They didn't exactly like the idea of having to pick up and move out of the homes their grandparents built. So pretty much the entire Middle East declared war on Israel the moment it was officially created. Israel won the war, but the bad blood, killing, and mutual hard feelings carry over to today.

Germany and Japan were basically vanquished and had to begin the long process of rebuilding. Germany was split in half, with East Germany under control of the Russians and West Germany becoming an independent country allied with the United States and Great Britain. Some of the top Nazis were put on trial for their crimes against humanity, and a few of them were executed. But for the most part they got to go on with their lives as normal, which is horrible and massively unfair if you think about it. The Russians weren't exactly kind to the East Germans (you can't really blame them), and conditions in East Germany got so bad the Russians had to build a big wall in the middle of Berlin to keep people from running over to West Germany to escape the Soviets (the east and west halves eventually joined back together in 1990). America put lots of money and energy into rebuilding West Germany and Japan, and both countries eventually came back bigger and better than ever. They're now powerful allies of the United States and Great Britain.

If you'd like to learn more about World War II, here are a couple of places where you can find good information online:

history.com

eyewitnesstohistory.com

You can also check out the bibliography in the back of this book to find books I used to do my research about World War II.

Vehicle Specifications for Aircraft Commonly Used During the War

Aircraft	Year	Speed (mph)	Weight (lbs)	Climb Rate (ft/min)	Ceiling (ft)	Crew	Machine Guns	Cannons
Germany								
Dornier Do-17 Bomber	1937	265	19,482	850	26,903	4	6x 7.92mm	
Messerschmitt Bf-109E-3	1939	350	5,875	3,200	34,451	1	2x 7.92mm	2x 20mm
Junkers Ju-87B Stuka	1939	255	12,880	1,094	26,245	2	3x 7.92mm	2x 20mm
Messerschmitt Bf-109G-10	1944	385	7,500	4,000	36,583	1	2x 13mm	1x 20mm
Focke-Wulf 190 A-8	1944	408	10,800	2,350	37,400	1	2x 13mm	4x 20mm
Messerschmitt Me-262 Jet	1944	559	14,272	3,900	37,565	1		4x 30mm
Japan								
Nakajima B5N Kate	1937	235	8,380	1,283	27,100	3	3x 7.7mm	
Aichi D3A1 Val	1939	242	8,047	1,869	30,500	2	3x 7.7mm	
Mitsubishi A6M2 Zero	1940	331	5,555	3,100	33,794	1	2x 7.7mm	2x 20mm
UK								
Hawker Hurricane Mk. I	1938	330	6,666	2,250	36,000	1	8x .303 cal	
Supermarine Spitfire Mk. I	1938	355	5,784	2,530	34,000	1	8x .303 cal	

Aircraft	Year	Speed (mph)	Weight (lbs)	Climb Rate (ft/min)	Ceiling (ft)	Crew	Machine Guns	Cannons
USA								
Grumman F4F-3 Wildcat	1940	330	7,467	2,050	32,600	1	4x .50 cal	
SBD Dauntless	1940	252	9,353	1,700	25,530	2	4x .50 cal	
Curtiss P-40B Warhawk	1941	352	7,326	2,860	32,400	1	4x .50 cal	
Boeing B-17G Flying Fortress	1941	287	54,000	900	35,600	10	12x .50 cal	
Republic P-47D Thunderbolt	1943	430	13,500	2,780	40,000	1	8x .50 cal	
Vought F4U-1A Corsair	1943	417	11,093	3,250	36,895	1	6x .50 cal	
Lockheed P38J Lightning	1943	420	17,500	2,850	44,000	1	4x .50 cal	1x 20mm
North American P-51D Mustang	1944	437	10,100	3,475	41,900	1	6x .50 cal	
Boeing B-29 Superfortress	1944	357	120,000	900	31,850	11	12x .50 cal	
USSR								
Polikarpov Po-2 Biplane	1929	94	2,271	546	9,843	2	1x 7.62mm	
Yakovlev Yak-1	1941	373	6,383	3,940	32,800	1	2x 12.7mm	1x 20mm
Ilyushin IL-2 Sturmovik	1941	257	14,065	2,050	18,045	2	3x 7.62mm	2x 23mm
Mikoyan-Gurevich MiG-3	1941	398	7,415	2,554	39,400	1	3x 7.62mm	

Vehicle Specifications for Tanks Commonly Used During the War

Tank	Year	Weight (tons)	Frontal Armor (mm)	Speed (mph)	Crew	Machine Gun	Main Cannon
Germany							
Panzer III	1939	25	30	25	5	2x 7.92mm	50mm KwK 38 L/42
Panzer IV	1939	28	50	25	5	2x 7.92mm	75mm KwK 37 L/24
StuG III	1940	26	80	25	4	1x 7.92mm	75mm StuK 40 L/48
Panzer IV Ausf H	1942	26	80	25	5	2x 7.92mm	75mm KwK 40 L/48
Pz. V Panther	1943	50	80	29	5	2x 7.92mm	75mm KwK 42 L/70
Pz. VI Tiger	1943	50	100	23	5	2x 7.92mm	88mm KwK 36 L/56
Pz. VIB Tiger II	1944	76	150	24	5	2x 7.92mm	88mm KwK 43 L/71
Japan							
Type 97 Chi-Ha	1936	16.5	28	24	4	2x 7.7mm	57mm Type 97
UK							
Mark II Matilda	1940	27	78	15	4	2x 7.92mm	40mm Ordnance QF 2-pdr
Mark IV Churchill	1941	39	102	17	5	2x 7.92mm	75mm Ordnance QF 6-pdr
Sherman Firefly	1944	39	85	25	5	1x .30-cal, 1x .50-cal	76.2mm Ordnance QF 17-pdr

Tank	Year	Weight (tons)	Frontal Armor (mm)	Speed (mph)	Crew	Machine Gun	Main Cannon
USA							
M3 Stuart	1940	14	43	36	4	3x .30-cal	37mm M5 L/50
M4A1 Sherman	1942	33	75	25	5	2x .30-cal, 1x .50-cal	75mm M3 L/40
M4A3E8 Sherman	1944	33	100	25	5	2x .30-cal, 1x .50-cal	76mm M1
USSR							
T-34/76	1940	30	45	32	4	2x 7.62mm	76.2mm M-40
T-34/85	1943	32	75	31	4	2x 7.62mm	85mm M-43
IS-2	1943	51	120	23	4	2x 7.62mm	122mm D25-T

ACKNOWLEDGMENTS

Writing a book is an adventure. To begin with it is a toy and an amusement. Then it becomes a mistress, then it becomes a master, then it becomes a tyrant. The last phase is that just as you are about to be reconciled to your servitude, you kill the monster and fling him to the public.

—Winston Churchilll

THIS BOOK IS DEDICATED TO MY FAMILY. OVER the course of my writing, I was faced with countless challenges coming at me from every conceivable direction, both professional and personal, yet every time things seemed insurmountable my family was there with smiles on their faces. I have said before that I can't do this without you guys, but never has that been more accurate than this time around!

It's dedicated to my amazing, beautiful, beloved wife, Simone. I'd have been a wreck without your endless support, your kindness, and your ability to constantly show me that family and love are the most important things in life. It's dedicated to my mom, who had a homemade quiche ready every time I felt like I'd fallen down and couldn't get back up again. It's dedicated to everyone in my life—my dad; my stepdaughter, Presley; my brothers, Clay and John; and my uncle Fred, all of whom came through for me every single time I needed them. And to my friends, Matt, Andrew, Brian, Manny, and the D&D crew, who kept me sane in a sea of insanity on levels I'll never fully be able to articulate.

I'd like to thank my amazing editor, Deirdre Jones, who has never been anything other than easygoing, understanding, and great to work with. Thanks also to my fact-checker, Jody Revenson, who was incredibly thorough in her efforts to keep me from turning this into too much of an action movie, and to my excellent agents, Farley Chase of Chase Literary and Sean Daily at Hotchkiss, for tirelessly working on promoting these books in every single direction and undertaking the heroic job of trying to make me seem cool and interesting and marketable somehow.

And lastly, I'd like to thank you, the readers, for your constant and incredibly awesome, over-the-top support. I love each and every one of you in a very nonweird platonic way, and that's a fact. I don't care what all those jerks say about you behind your back—you're always going to be cool with me.

BIBLIOGRAPHY

Education is a weapon whose effects depend on who holds it in his hands and at whom it is aimed.

—Josef Stalin

"Agansing Rai, VC." *The Telegraph*. May 30, 2000.

Agte, Patrick. *Michael Wittmann and the Waffen SS Tiger Commanders of the Leibstandarte in World War II*. Mechanicsburg, PA: Stackpole Books, 2006.

Alexander, Joseph H. *The Final Campaign: Marines in the Victory on Okinawa*. Washington, DC: Marine Corps Historical Center, 1996.

Alexander, Joseph H. *Storm Landings: Epic Amphibious Battles of the Central Pacific*. Annapolis, MD: Naval Institute Press, 1997.

Ambrose, Stephen E. *Band of Brothers*. New York: Touchstone, 2001.

Ambrose, Stephen E. *D-Day: June 6, 1944*. New York: Simon & Schuster, 1994.

Appleman, Roy Edgar, et al. *Okinawa: The Last Battle*. Washington, DC: Center of Military History, 2000.

Arostegui, Martin C. *Twilight Warriors*. New York: Macmillan, 1997.

Ashcroft, Michael. *Victoria Cross Heroes*. London: Headline Publishing Group, 2007.

Atwood, Kathryn J. *Women Heroes of World War II*. Chicago: Chicago Review Press, 2004.

Axelrod, Alan. *Encyclopedia of World War II*. New York: Facts on File, 2007.

Barbier, Mary. *D-Day Deception*. Westport, CT: Greenwood Press, 2007.

Bonner, Kermit. *Final Voyages*. Padukah, KY: Turner Publishing, 1997.

Boyne, Walter J. *Air Warfare.* Santa Barbara, CA: ABC-CLIO, 2002.

Braddon, Russell. *Nancy Wake.* Stroud, UK: Sutton Publishing Limited, 2005.

Breuer, William B. *Daring Missions of World War II.* New York: John Wiley & Sons, 2001.

Brinkley, Douglas. *The WWII Desk Reference.* New York: HarperCollins, 2004.

Brokaw, Tom. *The Greatest Generation.* New York: Random House, 2004.

Bull, Stephen. *Encyclopedia of Military Technology and Innovation.* Westport, CT: Greenwood Press, 2004.

Butler, Robert. *Legions of Death.* Barnsley, UK: Pen and Sword, 2004.

Caddick-Adams, Peter. *Monte Cassino: Ten Armies in Hell.* New York: Oxford University Press, 2013.

Caddick-Adams, Peter. *Snow and Steel: The Battle of the Bulge 1944–45.* New York: Oxford University Press, 2014.

Cawthorne, Nigel. *Military Commanders.* London: Enchanted Lion, 2004.

Chambers, John Whiteclay. *The Oxford Companion to American Military History.* New York: Oxford University Press, 1999.

Clark, Johnnie. *Gunner's Glory.* New York: Random House, 2004.

Clarke, John. *Gallantry Medals & Decorations of the World.* Barnsley, UK: Pen and Sword, 2001.

Collier, Peter, and Nick Del Calzo. *Medal of Honor.* New York: Artisan, 2011.

Cook, Bernard A. *Women and War.* Santa Barbara, CA: ABC-CLIO, 2006.

Coonts, Steven. *War in the Air.* New York: Simon & Schuster, 2003.

Cowley, Robert, and Geoffrey Parker. *The Reader's Companion to Military History.* New York: Houghton Mifflin, 1996.

Craig, William. *Enemy at the Gates.* London: Classic Penguin, 2000.

Cressman, Robert. *The Official Chronology of the US Navy in World War II.* Annapolis, MD: Naval Institute Press, 2000.

Crisp, Bob. *Brazen Chariots.* New York: W. W. Norton, 2005.

Crisp, Bob. *The Gods Were Neutral.* New York: W. W. Norton, 1961.

Davis, Paul K. *100 Decisive Battles from Ancient Times to the Present.* New York: Oxford University Press, 2001.

Dear, I. C. B., and M. R. D. Foot. *The Oxford Companion to World War II.* New York: Oxford University Press, 1995.

Delaforce, Patrick. *Battles with Panzers.* Stroud, UK: Sutton, 2003.

De Pauw, Linda Grant. *Battle Cries and Lullabies: Women in War from Prehistory to the Present.* Norman, OK: University of Oklahoma Press, 1998.

Douglas, Deborah G., et al. *American Women and Flight Since 1940.* Lexington, KY: University Press of Kentucky, 2004.

Duffy, C. *Red Storm on the Reich.* London: Routledge, 1991.

Duncan, Joyce. *Ahead of Their Time*. Westport, CT: Greenwood Press, 2002.

Farwell, Byron. *The Gurkhas*. New York: W. W. Norton, 1984.

Fiedler, Arkady. *303 Squadron: The Legendary Battle of Britain Fighter Squadron*. Translated by Jarek Garlinski. Los Angeles: Aquila Polonica, 2010.

Fitzsimmons, Bernard. *Heraldry and Regalia of War*. New York: Beekman House, 1973.

Forczyk, Robert. *Panther vs. T-34*. Oxford, UK: Osprey, 2007.

Ford, Daniel. *Flying Tigers*. New York: HarperCollins, 2010.

Foss, Clive. *The Tyrants*. London: Quercus, 2006.

Gandt, Robert. *The Twilight Warriors*. New York: Crown, 2010.

Giangreco, D. M. *Hell to Pay: Operation DOWNFALL and the Invasion of Japan*. Annapolis, MD: Naval Institute Press, 2009.

Goldstein, Donald M. *The Way It Was*. Washington, DC: Brassey's, 2001.

Goldstein, Richard. "Col. W. R. Lawley, Jr., 78, World War II Hero." *New York Times*. June 1, 1999.

Gruhl, Werner. *Imperial Japan's World War Two: 1931–1945*. New Brunswick, NJ: Transaction Publishers, 2007.

Haigh, Gideon. *Silent Revolutions*. Melbourne, VIC: Black Inc., 2006.

Heinz, W. C. *When We Were One*. New York: Basic Books, 2003.

Holt, Thaddeus. *The Deceivers*. New York: Skyhorse, 2007.

Horn, Bernd, and John Scott Cowan. *Intrepid Warriors*. Toronto, ONT: Dundurn Press, 2007.

Horner, David Murray, and Paul Collier. *The Second World War*. New York: Taylor & Francis, 2003.

Hart, Stephen A. *Sherman Firefly vs. Tiger*. Oxford, UK: Osprey, 2007.

Hawes, Allison. *Who's Who in WW2*. London: A&C Black, 2010.

Harmsen, Peter. *Shanghai 1937: Stalingrad on the Yangtze*. Havertown, PA: Casemate Publishers, 2013.

Heinemann, Sue. *Timelines of American Women's History*. New York: Penguin, 1996.

Hite, Kenneth. *The Nazi Occult*. Oxford, UK: Osprey, 2013.

Hopkins, William B. *The Pacific War*. Minneapolis: Zenith Press, 2008.

"Honour Sought for Hero Bear." *BBC News*. January 25, 2008.

Hornfischer, James D. *The Last Stand of the Tin Can Sailors*. New York: Bantam, 2004.

Hutchinson, James Lee. *The Boys in the B-17*. Bloomington, IN: Authorhouse, 2011.

Iggulden, Conn, and Hal Iggulden. *The Dangerous Book for Boys*. New York: HarperCollins, 2007.

Korda, Michael. *With Wings Like Eagles: The Untold Story of the Battle of Britain*. New York: Harper Perennial, 2002.

Kurowski, Franz. *Luftwaffe Aces*. Mechanicsburg, PA: Stackpole, 2004.

Laver, Harry S., and Jeffrey J. Matthews. *The Art of Command*. Lexington, KY: University of Kentucky Press, 2008.

Lawson, Dorothea von Schwanenfluegel, *Laughter Wasn't Rationed*. Medford, OR: Tricor Press, 1999.

Leckie, Robert. *Strong Men Armed: The United States Marines Against Japan*. Cambridge, MA: Da Capo Press, 2010.

Leonov, Viktor. *Blood on the Shores*. New York: Ivy, 1994.

Lewis, John E. *The Mammoth Book of How It Happened: World War II*. London: Robinson, 2002.

Li, Xiobing. *China at War: An Encyclopedia*. Santa Barbara, CA: ABC-CLIO, 2012.

Libby, Leona Woods Marshall. *The Uranium People*. New York: Crane, Russak, 1979.

Lucas, J. *Last Days of the Reich*. London: Grafton, 1987.

Luto, James. *Fighting with the Fourteenth Army in Burma*. Barnsley, UK: Pen and Sword, 2013.

MacDonald, John. *Great Battlefields of the World*. New York: Collier Books, 1985.

MacDonald, John. *Great Battles of World War II*. New York: Macmillan, 1986.

Macklin, Robert. *Bravest*. Crows Nest, NSW: Allen & Unwin, 2008.

Mallett, Ashley. *Eleven*. St. Lucia, QLD: University of Queensland Press, 2001.

Martin, Jonathan. *World War II in HD Colour*. World Media Rights, 2008–2009.

Miles, Rosalind, and Robin Cross. *Hell Hath No Fury: True Profiles of Women in War from Antiquity to Iraq*. New York: Three Rivers Press, 2004.

Millman, Nicholas. *Ki-27 Nate Aces*. Oxford, UK: Osprey, 2013.

Milner, Mark. *Battle of the Atlantic*. Stroud, UK: History Press, 2011.

Mitter, Rana. *Forgotten Ally: China's World War II, 1937–1945*. New York: Houghton Mifflin, 2013.

Morison, Samuel Eliot. *History of United States Naval Operations in World War II*. Urbana, IL: University of Illinois Press, 2001.

Mueller, Joseph N. *Guadalcanal 1942*. Oxford, UK: Osprey, 1992.

Nabokov, Peter. *Native American Testimony*. New York: Penguin, 1999.

Nadler, John. *A Perfect Hell*. New York: Random House, 2007.

Noggle, Anne, and Christine A. White. *A Dance with Death*. College Station, TX: Texas A&M University Press, 2001.

Norris, John. *World War II Trucks and Tanks*. Stroud, UK: Spellmount, 2012.

Ogilvie, Marilyn Bailey, and Joy Dorothy Harvey. *The Biographical Dictionary of Women in Science*. New York: Taylor & Francis, 2000.

Olson, James S. *Historical Dictionary of the Great Depression, 1929–1940.* Westport, CT: Greenwood Press, 2001.

Paige, Mitchell. *A Marine Named Mitch.* New York: Vantage, 1975.

Parker, Danny S. *The Battle of the Bulge: Hitler's Ardennes Offensive.* Cambridge, MA: Da Capo, 2004.

Paul, Louis. *Tales from the Cult Film Trenches.* Jefferson, NC: McFarland, 2008.

Pennington, Reina, and John Erickson. *Wings, Women, and War.* Lawrence, KS: University of Kansas, 2007.

Pilecki, Witold. *The Auschwitz Survivor.* Translated by Jarek Garlinski. Los Angeles: Aquila Polonica, 2012.

Plunka, Gene A. *Staging Holocaust Resistance.* New York: Palgrave Macmillan, 2012.

Polmar, Norman, and Thomas B. Allen. *World War II: Encyclopedia of the War Years, 1941–1945.* Boston: Houghton Mifflin, 2012.

Pujol, Juan, and Nigel West. *Garbo.* London: Grafton, 1986.

Putney, Martha S. *Blacks in the United States Army.* Jefferson, NC: McFarland, 2003

Qiaoqi. "Last Chinese War Hero Suffers Destitution and Insult." *Epoch Times.* February 2, 2011.

Rankin, Nicholas. *A Genius for Deception.* Oxford, UK: Oxford University Press, 2009.

Rashke, Richard. *Escape from Sobibor.* New York: Open Road Media, 2012.

Robinson, Gary, and Phil Lucas. *From Warriors to Soldiers.* New York: iUniverse, 2010.

Rottman, Gordon L. *Okinawa 1945: The Last Battle.* Oxford, UK: Osprey, 2003.

Rudel, Hans-Ulrich. *Stuka Pilot.* New York: Ballantine, 1958.

Ryan, Cornelius. *A Bridge Too Far.* New York: Simon & Schuster, 1974.

Ryan, Cornelius. *The Last Battle.* New York: Touchstone, 1995.

Sakaida, Henry. *Heroes of the Soviet Union 1941–45.* Oxford, UK: Osprey, 2004.

Sakaida, Henry. *Heroines of the Soviet Union.* Oxford, UK: Osprey, 2003.

Sakaida, Henry. *Japanese Army Air Aces 1937–45.* Oxford, UK: Osprey, 1997.

Sandler, Stanley. *Ground Warfare: An International Encyclopedia.* 3 vols. Santa Barbara, CA: ABC-CLIO, 2002.

Sanger, S. L. *Working on the Bomb.* Portland, OR: Continuing Education Press, 1995.

Scheibert, Horst. *The Panther Family.* Atglen, PA: Schiffer Publishing, 1990.

Schneider, Carl J., and Dorothy Schneider. *World War II.* New York: Checkmark, 2003.

Scholey, Pete, and Frederick Forsyth. *Who Dares Wins.* Oxford, UK: Osprey, 2008.

Sealey, D. Bruce, and Peter Van De Vyvre. *Manitobans in Profile.* New York: Penguin, 1981.

Showalter, Dennis E. *Armor and Blood: The Battle of Kursk*. New York: Random House, 2013.

Seaman, Mark. *Garbo: The Spy Who Saved D-Day*. Toronto, ONT: Dundurn Press, 2004.

Shortt, James. *The Special Air Service*. Oxford, UK: Osprey, 1981.

Shugaar, Anthony, and Steven Guarnaccia. *I Lie for a Living*. Washington, DC: National Geographic, 2006.

Sinton, Starr, and Robert Hargis. *World War II Medal of Honor Recipients (2): Army and Air Corps*. Oxford, UK: Osprey, 2003.

Sledge, E. B. *With the Old Breed: At Peleliu and Okinawa*. New York: Presidio Press, 2007.

Smith, Carl. *Pearl Harbor 1941*. Oxford, UK: Osprey, 2001.

Smith, Larry, and Norman Schwarzkopf. *Beyond Glory*. New York: W. W. Norton, 2004.

Smith, Melvin Charles. *Awarded for Valour*. New York: Macmillan, 2008.

Sorley, Lewis. *Thunderbolt: General Creighton Abrams and the Army of His Times*. New York: Simon & Schuster, 1992.

Stahl, Peter. *Panzer: German Armor 1935–1945*. Santa Clara, CA: AAA Printers, 1970.

Strebe, Amy Goodpaster. *Flying for Her Country*. Santa Barbara, CA: Greenwood Publishing Group, 2007.

Stronge, Charles. *Kill Shot*. Berkeley, CA: Ulysses Press, 2011.

Takemae, Eiji, and Robert Ricketts. *Allied Occupation of Japan*. New York: Continuum, 2003.

Tillman, Barrett. *Wildcat Aces of World War 2*. Oxford, UK: Osprey, 1995.

Timofeyeva-Yegorova, Anna. *Red Sky, Black Death*. Bloomington, IN: Slavica, 2009.

Travers, Susan. *Tomorrow Be Brave*. New York: Free Press, 2001.

Tucker, Spencer C. *Encyclopedia of World War I*. Santa Barbara, CA: ABC-CLIO, 2005.

Walsh, George J. "Smoke and Battle of Midway." United States Naval Institute. http://blog.usni.org/2009/09/26/flightdeck-friday-smoke-and-the-battle-of-midway. Retrieved October 8, 2014.

Watson, Brent Byron. *Far Eastern Tour*. Montreal, QBC: McGill-Queen's, 2002.

Wayne, Tiffany K. *American Women of Science Since 1900*. Santa Barbara, CA: ABC-CLIO, 2011.

Weale, Adrian. *Army of Evil*. New York: New American Library, 2012.

Weal, John. *Ju 87 Stukageschwader Aces of the Russian Front*. Oxford, UK: Osprey, 2008.

Willbanks, James H. *America's Heroes*. Santa Barbara, CA: ABC-CLIO, 2011.

Williamson, Gordon. *Knight's Cross with Diamonds Recipients*. Oxford, UK: Osprey, 2006.

Williamson, Gordon. *The Waffen-SS (1): 1 to 5 Divisions*. Oxford, UK: Osprey, 2003.

Wilson, Joe. *The 761st "Black Panther" Tank Battalion in World War II*. Jefferson, NC: McFarland, 1999.

Wright, Michael. *What They Didn't Teach You About WWII*. New York: Random House, 2009.

"Xie Jinyuan." China Central Television. www.cctv.com/lm/176/71/88857.html. Retrieved August 25, 2013.

Yenne, Bill. *Aces High*. New York: Penguin, 2010.

Yenne, Bill. *Big Week: Six Days that Changed the Course of World War II*. New York: Penguin, 2012.

Young, Edward M. *Meiktila 1945*. Oxford, UK: Osprey, 2004.

Zabecki, David T. *World War II in Europe*. New York: Taylor & Francis, 1999.

Zaitsev, Vasily. *Notes of a Russian Sniper*. Translated by David Givens, Peter Kornakov, and Konstantin Kornakov. London: Frontline Books, 2009.

Zaloga, Steven. *T-34/76 Medium Tank 1941–45*. Oxford, UK: Osprey, 2013.

PHOTO CREDITS

p. 4: Courtesy of the German Federal Archives. p. 44: Courtesy of the German Federal Archives. p. 45: Courtesy of the German Federal Archives. p. 56: Courtesy of the Imperial War Museums. p. 60: Courtesy of the Royal Air Force Museum. p. 91: Courtesy of the Franklin D. Roosevelt Presidential Library and Museum. p. 107: Courtesy of the Imperial War Museums. p. 113: Courtesy of the Imperial War Museums. p. 130: Courtesy of the United States Navy. p. 131: Courtesy of the United States Navy. p. 143: Courtesy of the German Federal Archives. p. 155: Courtesy of the United States Marine Corps. p. 163 left: Courtesy of the United States Marine Corps. p. 163 right: Courtesy of the United States Marine Corps. p. 172: Natalia Fedorovna Bode, Courtesy of the Russian International News Agency. p. 173: Courtesy of the German Federal Archives. p. 174: Courtesy of the German Federal Archives. p. 188: Courtesy of Rafał M. Socha. p. 203: Courtesy of the Imperial War Museums. p. 207: Courtesy of the Imperial War Museums. p. 217: Courtesy of the United States Air Force. p. 221: US Office for Emergency Management, Courtesy of the National Archives and Records Administration. p. 234: Courtesy of the Australian War Memorial. p. 239: Courtesy of Library and Archives Canada. p. 250: Courtesy of the National Archives and Records Administration. p. 253: Courtesy of the National Archives and Records Administration. p. 271: Captain Keating, No. 2 Army Film and Photographic Unit, Courtesy of the Imperial War Museums. p. 283: Courtesy of the United States Navy. p. 286: Courtesy of the United States Navy National Museum of Naval Aviation. p. 291: US Army Private William Roof, Courtesy of the United States Army Signal Corps Collection. p. 299: Courtesy of the United States Army Center for Military History. p. 307: Courtesy of the United States Army. p. 308: Courtesy of Ad Meskens. p. 314: Courtesy of the Imperial War Museums. p. 321: Courtesy of the Imperial War Museums. p. 330: Courtesy of the United States Navy. p. 331: Private Bob Bailey, Courtesy of the United States Marine Corps. p. 335: Staff Sergeant Walter F. Kleine, Courtesy of the National Archives and Records Administration.

INDEX